T0276298

"When two en-Spirited people, wife and husband, join to offer their gifts of writing and art in a single volume, the blessing is doubled for readers. As David and Phaedra Taylor share in this book what moves and inspires them, it will speak into your heart and mind as their words and images rise from the page to enrich you."

Luci Shaw, writer-in-residence at Regent College and author of *Reversing Entropy*

"*Prayers for the Pilgrimage* is a thoughtful and delightful pairing of perceptive petitions and sensitive paintings, designed to tune the mind and heart to whispers of the eternal hidden in the everyday."

Douglas McKelvey, author of *Every Moment Holy, Volumes I and II*

"I'm so grateful for the work of David and Phaedra Taylor, as they both point us toward the heart of the Lord. May we all draw closer to the beauty of the Lord through these prayers and paintings."

Jamie Ivey, author and host of the podcast, *The Happy Hour with Jamie Ivey*

"This collection of beautifully crafted collects—little prayers for all kinds of occasions, encounters, dilemmas, and moments of celebration—will be a welcome resource for Christians everywhere. These prayers are deeply rooted in Scripture and yet speak powerfully into modern life. Many of them are memorable, beauty crafted little prose poems that will stay with the reader long after they have first been prayed. These prayers are indeed a host of good companions for life's pilgrimage."

Malcolm Guite, poet and author of *Mariner: A Theological Voyage with Samuel Taylor Coleridge*

"I thank God for *Prayers for the Pilgrimage*. Prayer is the root system that feeds and nurtures our life with God. Author W. David O. Taylor has provided us with just such a root system. Watercolor paintings by Phaedra J. Taylor placed at the beginning of each section are a lovely addition to this collection. They encourage us to pause in our reading and praying for quiet reflection and meditation . . . a *selah*, to use the language of the Psalms. *Prayers for the Pilgrimage* is a treasure. Get it. Read it. Pray it."

Richard J. Foster, author of *Celebration of Discipline* and *Learning Humility*

"Sometimes we have all the words to pray. Sometimes we don't have any. This book is a perfect companion for the seasons when we could use some help with what we really want to say."
Scott Erickson, author of *Honest Advent* and *Say Yes*

"This collection of short, nuanced prayers is a gift that points us to the deep love God has not only for us but for our neighbors too. David Taylor offers thoughtful words for the journey, lending us prayers for a multitude of occasions, celebrations, and pain points, inviting us to bring our whole selves to the One who hears every cry of our hearts. This beautiful book is a rich resource for individuals, families, and churches, reminding us of God's presence in the joys and sorrows of life together."
Kayla Craig, author of *Every Season Sacred* and *To Light Their Way: A Collection of Prayers and Liturgies for Parents*

"Inherited prayers from our foremothers and forefathers in the faith have long helped Christians celebrate, mourn, survive, and simply live into the church's rhythms of marking time. *Prayers for the Pilgrimage* brings a fresh perspective to this long-standing Christian practice. The words and images within its pages lay bare the human heart and the very heart of God in a time when prayers that draw us near to God and to one another in community are desperately needed. Wherever one is on their faith journey, *Prayers for the Pilgrimage* will give voice to the varied and complex needs of life in the twenty-first century."
Teesha Hadra, rector of Church of the Resurrection Los Angeles

W. DAVID O. TAYLOR
with paintings by
PHAEDRA TAYLOR

Prayers

for the

PILGRIMAGE

A BOOK *of* COLLECTS

for ALL *of* LIFE

An imprint of InterVarsity Press
Downers Grove, Illinois

InterVarsity Press
P.O. Box 1400 | Downers Grove, IL 60515-1426
ivpress.com | email@ivpress.com

InterVarsity Press® is the publishing division of InterVarsity Christian Fellowship/USA®. For more information, visit intervarsity.org.

The following prayers first appeared in W. David O. Taylor, "15 Prayers for a Violent World," *Christianity Today*, May 27, 2022, https://www.christianitytoday.com/ct/2022/may-web-only/prayer-for-school-shooting-police -war-lament-violence.html: For the Visit of the Magi, For Palm Sunday, From the Fear of Death, For Police Officers, Of Allegiance to the Prince of Peace, For Peace in a Time of War, For Those Who Weary of Doing Justice, To Become a Justice-Loving People, Against Bloodthirstiness, For Enemies, After a Mass Shooting, A Prayer for Loving a Hurting Neighbor, A Prayer Against Neighbor Hate.

The following prayers first appeared in W. David O. Taylor, "11 Back-to-School Prayers," *Christianity Today*, August 26, 2020, https://www.christianitytoday.com/ct/2020/august-web-only/11-back-to-school-prayers -for-parents-students-and-teachers.html: "O Lord, you who guide me in the hours of the day and guard me through the watches of the night," "O God, you who make new again and again," Against a Plague, For Parents Sending their Children off to a New School, For School Administrators, For Oneself as a Teacher, For High School and College Students, For Homeschooled Kids, For Children Going to School, Before a Hard Meeting.

The publisher cannot verify the accuracy or functionality of website URLs used in this book beyond the date of publication.

Cover design: David Fassett
Interior design: Daniel van Loon
Images: Phaedra Taylor

ISBN 978-1-5140-0823-2 (print) | ISBN 978-1-5140-0824-9 (digital)

Printed in the United States of America ∞

Library of Congress Cataloging-in-Publication Data
A catalog record for this book is available from the Library of Congress.

31 30 29 28 27 26 25 24 | 12 11 10 9 8 7 6 5 4 3 2 1

To Blythe and Sebastian:

"Stand at the crossroads and look, and ask for the ancient paths,
where the good way lies; and walk in it,
and find rest for your souls."

CONTENTS

Introduction/ 1

Prayers for Life: Artist Statement by
Phaedra Taylor/ 19

PRAYERS FOR MORNING AND EVENING

Morning Prayers/ 25

Evening Prayers/ 27

PRAYERS FOR MONDAY TO SUNDAY

For Monday ("Moon Day")/ 31

For Tuesday ("Tiw's Day")/ 32

For Wednesday ("Woden's Day")/ 32

For Thursday ("Thor's Day")/ 32

For Friday ("Frigg's Day")/ 32

For Saturday 1 ("Saturn's Day")/ 33

For Saturday 2 ("sábado")/ 33

For Sunday 1 ("Sun's Day")/ 33

For Sunday 2 ("domingo")/ 34

PRAYERS FOR THE SECULAR CALENDAR

For New Year's Day/ 37

For the Feast of Saint Valentine/ 37

For a Lonely Valentine's Day/ 37

For MLK Jr. Day (For the Dignity of
All People)/ 38

For MLK Jr. Day (For Being a People
of Peace)/ 38

For Memorial Day/ 39

For Mother's Day/ 39

For Father's Day/ 39

For Juneteenth/ 40

For Independence Day/ 40

For Halloween (For Joy and
Festivity)/ 40

For Halloween (For the Defeat of all
Evils)/ 41

For the Thanksgiving of Good
Things/ 41

For the Thanksgiving of Hard
Things/ 42

For Christmas Eve/ 42

For Sanity on Christmas Eve for
Frazzled Parents/ 42

For New Year's Eve (For a Good
Ending)/ 43

For New Year's Eve (For a Hard
Ending)/ 43

PRAYERS FOR THE CHURCH CALENDAR

Prayers for Advent

Prayers of Light/ 45

Prayers of Hope/ 46

Prayers of Joy/ 48

Prayers of Trust/ 49

For Saint Nicholas Day
(December 6)/ 51

For Saint Lucia Day
(December 13)/ 51

For the Virgin Mary/ 51

For Saint Joseph/ 52

Prayers for Christmastide

For the First Day of Christmas/ 52

For the Second Day of Christmas
(Saint Stephen's Day,
December 26)/ 52

For the Third Day of Christmas
(Saint John the Apostle's Day,
December 27)/53
For the Fourth Day of Christmas
(Feast of the Holy Innocents,
December 28)/53
For the Fifth Day of Christmas/53
For the Sixth Day of Christmas/54
For the Seventh Day of Christmas/54
For the Eighth Day of Christmas
(Feast of the Circumcision of
Christ, January 1)/54
For the Ninth Day of Christmas
(Feast of the Holy Name)/55
For the Tenth Day of Christmas/55
For the Eleventh Day of
Christmas/55
For the Twelfth Day of Christmas/56

Prayers for Epiphanytide

For the Visit of the Magi/56
For Growing in Wisdom/56
For the Flight to Egypt/57
For the Feast of the Baptism of Our
Lord (January 8)/57
For Shrove Tuesday/57

Prayers for Lent

For Ash Wednesday/58
For the First Sunday of Lent/58
For the Second Sunday of Lent/59
For the Third Sunday of Lent/59
For the Fourth Sunday of Lent/59
For the Fifth Sunday of Lent/60
For Palm Sunday/60
For Holy Monday/61
For Holy Tuesday/61
For Holy Wednesday/61
For Maundy Thursday/62
For Good Friday/62
For Holy Saturday/62

Prayers for Eastertide

For the First Sunday of Eastertide/63
For the Second Sunday of
Eastertide/63
For the Third Sunday of
Eastertide/63
For the Fourth Sunday of
Eastertide/64
For the Fifth Sunday of Eastertide/64
For the Sixth Sunday of
Eastertide/64
For the Seventh Sunday of
Eastertide/65
For Ascension Day (to Be Prayed the
Fortieth Day After Easter)/65

Prayers for Pentecost

For the Harmony of Christ's
Discordant Body/65
For the Fire of God to Become a Fire
in Our Bones/66

*Prayers for the End of the
Church Year*

For Trinity Sunday (to Be Prayed on
the Sunday After Pentecost)/66
For All Saints' Day (November 1)/66
For All Souls Day (November 2)/67
For Christ the King Sunday/67

**PRAYERS FOR BIRTH
TO DEATH**

For the Birth of a Child/69
For One's Own Birthday/69
For Another's Birthday/70
For the Adoption of a Child/70
For the Beginning of a New Season
of Life/71
For the Ending of a Season of Life/71
For a Midlife Crisis/72
For Aging Well/72

For an Untimely Death/73
For Gratitude in the Death of a
Beloved One/73
For the Fear of Death/74

**PRAYERS FOR JOY
AND SORROW**

For the Triple Power of Joy/77
For a Good Surprise/77
For the Joyful Life of Jesus/77
After a Great Victory/78
After a Hard Defeat/78
For Joy when It Is Hard to Come
By/78
For Feeling Low/79
For a Beleaguered Heart/79
For Those Who Don't Feel Loved by
God/79
For Being Mad at God/80
For Parents Whose Children Have
Abandoned the Faith/80
For Those Suffering from
Dementia/81
For Anger/81
For Sadness/81
For Being Stressed Out (After Saint
Basil)/82
For God's Ear to Be Inclined to the
Hurting/82
For Tired Hearts/82
For Losing Out on an
Opportunity/82
For Perpetual and Painful
Waiting/83

**PRAYERS FOR SICKNESS
AND HEALING**

For the Healing of the Body/85
For Those Who Are Chronically
Sick or in Pain/85
For a Child in Need of Healing/86

For the Healing of a Family
Member/86
For Those Who Suffer in Their
Bodies/86
Before a Surgery/87
For Thanksgiving in the Healing of
a Body/87
For Being Instruments of God's
Healing in the World/88
For Those Who Struggle with
Mental Health/88
For Those Who Have Suffered
Trauma/88
For an Aging Body/89
Against a Plague/89

**PRAYERS FOR THE
VIRTUES AND VICES**

The Seven Virtues

For Faith/91
For Hope/91
For Love/92
For Prudence/92
For Fortitude/92
For Temperance/93
For Justice/93

The Seven Vices

For Pride/93
For Anger/94
For Envy/94
For Lust/94
For Sloth/95
For Greed/95
For Gluttony/96

PRAYERS FOR WORK

For a Blessing of the Day's Work/99
For the Consecration of One's Body
for the Labors of the Day/100

For Strength to Accomplish Impossible Tasks/ 100
For Good Labor when You Do Not Feel Like Laboring but You Need to Get Things Done/ 100
For Grace to Make the Best of this Day/ 101
For Those in Business/ 101
For Minding Our Own Business/ 101
For Janitors and Cleaners/ 102
For International Workers' Day/ 102
For Poll Workers/ 102
For Monotonous Work/ 103
For Administrative Work/ 103
For Writing a Sermon/ 103
For Getting Something Published, Produced, or Picked/ 104
For When Nothing Goes According to Plan/ 104
For Letting Go of All the Woulda, Coulda, Shouldas/ 105
For the Blessing of Small Labors/ 105
For Grocers/ 105
For Police Officers/ 106
For a Doctor/ 106
For Pastors/ 107
For Ministers/ 107
For Athletes/ 107
For Those Who Work with Their Hands/ 108

PRAYERS FOR CREATIVES

For the Blessing of the Father/ 111
For the Blessing of the Son/ 111
For the Blessing of the Spirit/ 112
For Help in the Face of Fears/ 112
For Help in the Face of Failures/ 112
For Help in the Face of Foes/ 113
For the Blessing of the Holy Trinity/ 113

PRAYERS FOR SCHOOL

For Children Going to School/ 115
For Homeschooled Kids/ 115
For High School and College Students/ 115
For Teachers/ 116
For Oneself as a Teacher/ 116
For School Administrators/ 117
For Parents Sending Their Children Off to a New School/ 117
Before Taking a Test/ 117
Before Grading a Test or a Paper/ 118
For Graduates/ 118

PRAYERS FOR MUNDANE LIFE

For Beginnings/ 121
For God's Daily Care/ 121
Before a Meal/ 122
For Discerning the Will of God/ 122
For Those Who Feel Vulnerable/ 122
For the Blessing of Little Deeds of Faith/ 123
For Knowing When to Say No to One More Thing That You Want to Do, Because It Will Probably Be Bad for Your Mental, Physical, and Relational Health/ 123
For a Sporting Game (After Nick Comiskey)/ 123
For When Things Don't Go According to Plan/ 124
For the One Who Feels Disoriented in Life/ 124
For Bleary-Eyed Parents/ 124
After a Restless Night of Sleep/ 125
In the Aftermath of a Bad Dream/ 125
For Not Doing Great Things for God (After Douglas McKelvey)/ 126
Against Living in an Economy of Scarcity/ 126

For Being Need-full of God/126
For Things that Seem
    Impossible/127
For Being Wise to Say No/127
For Making Broth/127
For a Day That's Going Only
    Wrong/128
For the Proper Numbering of Our
    Days/128
For the Little Things/128
For Little Deeds of Kindness to
    Another/129
For a Grumpy Mood/129
For Changing a Diaper at Night/129
For Getting Shots at the Doctor/130
For the Blessing of All My Senses/130
For Going on Vacation (After Ray
    Simpson)/130
For Thanksgiving on Behalf of
    Those Who Are Faithful in the
    Little Things/131
For Being Present to the Present/131
For Mere Mortals Like
    Ourselves/132
For Daily Bread/132
For a Job Interview/132
For Exhausted Mothers and
    Fathers/133
For a Conference/133
For Journeying to a New Home/134
Against "Settling" in Life/134
For Silence/134
For Endings/135

PRAYERS FOR PUBLIC LIFE

For Being Heralds of Good News/137
For Reading the Not-So-Good
    News/137
To Be Said After Reading Bad
    News/137
For Driving in Traffic/138

For Being Virtuous on Social
    Media/138
For Being Like the Care-Filled
    Jesus/138
For Not Being Ashamed of Jesus in
    Public/139
For Those Experiencing Food
    Insecurity/139
For the Installation of a New Head
    of State/140
For the Political Tempests of Our
    World/140
For Our Wounded Country/140
For Grace Between Fellow Believers
    Across Political Lines/141
For 9/11/141
For the Victims of War/141
For the War-Weary/142
For the Welfare of Our Cities/142
Against the Uproar of the
    Nations/142
For the Blessing of the Nations/143

PRAYERS FOR
RELATIONAL LIFE

For Speaking a Word of Blessing to
    All Whom I Meet/145
For Unity (After Psalm 133)/145
For the Gift of Good
    Community/145
For the Beloved Community/146
For Seeing Each Other as a Provision
    of Grace/146
For Single Parents/146
For Strained Relationships/147
For Grace in the Face of Contentious
    Relationships/147
For a Strained Christmas Day
    Family Meal/147
For a Strained Family
    Thanksgiving/148

xii ✄ *Contents*

For Those Who Do Not Feel at
  Home in Their Own Family/148
For Enduring Hard Things with
  Extended Family Members/148
For Reconciliation with a Fellow
  Believer/149
For the Blessing of a Marriage/149
For a Bad Patch in a Marriage/149
For a Struggling Marriage/150
For the Newly Divorced/150
For the Forgiveness of Sin Against
  One's Neighbor/150
For Strength to Forgive Those Who
  Have Hurt Us/151
For Struggling to Ask for
  Forgiveness/151
For the Blessing of One's Friends/151
For Being a True Friend/152
Before a Hard Conversation with a
  Friend/152
For the Friendless/152
For the Lonely Single Person/153
For a Hard Conversation Between
  Pastor and Parishioner/153
Before a Hard Meeting/153
For Being Delivered from What-
  about-ism/154
To Be Merciful Rather than
  Vindictive/154
For the Blessing of a Retreat/155

PRAYERS FOR A
VIOLENT WORLD

After a Mass Shooting/157
For Enemies/157
Against Bloodthirstiness/158
Against Our Own Violent
  Impulses/158
To Become a Justice-Loving
  People/158
For Those Who Weary of Doing
  Justice/159

For Peace in a Time of War/159
Of Allegiance to the Prince of
  Peace/159

PRAYERS FOR THE
LOVE OF NEIGHBOR

For Blessing Our Neighbor/161
For Seeing the Face of Christ in
  Our Neighbor/161
For Kindness to a Difficult
  Neighbor/161
Against Bearing False Witness/162
For Refugees/162
For the Release of Bitterness Against
  One's Neighbor/163
Against Neighbor Hate/163
For Loving a Hurting Neighbor/163
For Being Generous to One's
  Neighbor/164
Against Miserliness Toward One's
  Neighbor/164
For Loving Your Neighbor when
  You Don't Feel Like Loving
  Them/164

PRAYERS FOR
THE LOVE OF SELF

For Loving Ourself as We Have
  Loved Our Neighbors/167
For Being Patient with Oneself/167
For Being Kind Toward Oneself/167
For Not Being Proud of Oneself/168
For Not Dishonoring Oneself/168
For Not Being Self-Seeking in
  Oneself/168
For Not Being Easily Angered
  Toward Oneself/169
For Keeping No Record of Wrong
  Against Oneself/169

For Cherishing Goodness in
Oneself/ 169
For Believing All Things/ 170

PRAYERS FOR THE LOVE OF GOD

For Learning to Pray Afresh/ 173
For Those Who Have Lost the Will
to Pray/ 173
For Those Who Struggle to Be
Consistent in Prayer/ 174
For Not Wanting to Go to
Church/ 174
For the Renewal of the
Church/ 174
For the Anxious of Heart/ 175
For the Wearied and Worn
Down/ 175
For Physically Separated
Worship/ 175
Against Self-Deception/ 176
For Hungering for
Righteousness/ 176
For Being Childlike in God's
Kingdom/ 176
For Doubting Hearts/ 177
For the Cynics and Skeptics/ 177
For Those Who Have Only a
Flickering of Faith, Hope, and
Love/ 177
Against the Temptations of the Evil
One/ 178
For Those Who Are Dry in Their
Souls/ 178
For Not Giving Up on the Painful
Work of Becoming Whole and
Holy/ 178
For Those Who Feel Lost in Their
Own Selves/ 179
For Being the Light of the World/ 179
For Seeing What God Sees/ 179

For God's Self-Disclosure to Those
Who Are in Need/ 180
For Having the Eyes and Ears of
Christ/ 180
For Being One Hundred Percent
Honest with God/ 180
Against Stingy-Heartedness/ 181
For a Life of Integrity/ 181
For Making Forgiveness a Habit/ 181
For Deliverance from All Harm/ 182
For God's Judgment/ 182
For Being an Open Book to God/ 182
For Shelter from the Storms of
Life/ 183
For Vacation Bible School/ 183
For the Renovation of the Heart/ 183
For Protection from Abandonment
in the Face of the Perils of this
World/ 184
For Protection Against Our Mortal
Enemy/ 184
For Grace in the Face of
Suffering/ 184
For Fasting/ 185
For Being a Hot Mess Before God/ 185
For the Love of God/ 185

NATURE PRAYERS

For Taking Pleasure in God's
Creation/ 187
For Pets/ 187
For Green Spaces/ 188
For the Feast of Saint Francis
(October 4)/ 188
For a Bitterly Cold Morning/ 188
For a Miserably Hot Day/ 189
For Better Weather/ 189
For the Winter Solstice/ 189
For the Summer Solstice/ 190
Against Raging Hurricane
Storms/ 190

Against Raging Forest Fires/ 190
Against Raging Earthquakes/ 191
For the Care of Creation/ 191

CHILDREN'S PRAYERS

For God's Shepherding Care/ 193
For Waking Up on the Wrong Side
  of the Bed/ 194
For Bedtime/ 194
For Anxious Children at
  Bedtime/ 195

CELTIC PRAYERS

For a Blessing of the Day/ 197
For the Morning/ 197

For Commending Ourselves Wholly
  to Christ/ 198
For Being the Limbs of Christ/ 199
For Marriages/ 200
For Commending Our Night to
  Christ/ 200
To the Holy Trinity/ 201

A PRAYER FOR THE NOBODIES OF THE WORLD/ 203

Acknowledgments/ 205
Appendix: How to Write Your Own
  Collects/ 207

INTRODUCTION

I began writing collect prayers, or what is simply called a "collect," on March 15, 2020—the day that our country shut down on account of the coronavirus. At first, it was simply a way for me to cope with my own fears over an uncertain future. I'd written such prayers here and there, and I'd assigned them over the years to my students at Fuller Theological Seminary, but I now wrote them as a kind of daily spiritual exercise, and a rather desperate one.

I wrote a prayer titled "Against the Pestilence that Stalks in the Dark," giving voice to the language of Psalm 91, which prior to Covid-19 may have felt like something that only medieval Europeans suffering from the bubonic plague would have understood, but which now made immediate sense to us as a twenty-first-century global people. The archaic language of the King James Bible never felt so apt:

Thou shalt not be afraid . . .
for the pestilence that walketh in darkness;
nor for the destruction that wasteth at noonday.
(Psalm 91:5-6)

I wrote a prayer "For Dashed Plans" because it became increasingly obvious that there would be plenty of those to deal with in the months to come, resulting for some in bitter disappointment, for others in relief, grateful that they no longer needed to organize anything, at least for the foreseeable future. I wrote prayers "For Beleaguered Parents," among whom I counted myself, and "For Anxious Children," including my own, who often lacked the capacity to verbally name the jumble of feelings that roiled beneath the surface of their conscious understanding. I wrote a prayer "For the Depressed" after hearing of the experiences of the elderly, like my uncle, trapped in their nursing home rooms, confused and afraid; and of single people who lived alone in their apartments without any opportunities for meaningful physical touch from others.

I also wrote a prayer "Against Neighbor Hate" after the 2020 election, hoping it might arrest an impulse that had become all too easy to indulge for many of us in America.

For me, the writing of such prayers became a way to make sense of the realities of our world in upheaval.

In time, I began to receive messages from both friends and strangers, often through social media, requesting prayers on behalf of people who deserved our very best intercessions: "For Grocers Managing Panic-Buying Shoppers," "For Medical Professionals Overwhelmed by the Countless Sick," "For Garbage Collectors Working Overtime," and "For Untimely Deaths."

When schools began to open their doors again, my bishop asked if I might consider writing a series of "Back to School Prayers," which I did, keeping in mind the unique challenges faced not only by students but also by teachers and administrators. I published a separate batch of "Prayers for a Violent World" because our world had turned increasingly savage.

With my wife, Phaedra, a visual artist, I conceived a series of illustrated prayers that might allow people to pray not just with words but also with images—to see the shape of sorrow, to imagine the texture of death, or to perceive the beauty of feet that chose to publish peace instead of hate. For this particular venture, Phaedra and I created three sets of prayer cards for the Rabbit Room, a marvelous organization committed to cultivating creativity through community and artmaking.

Often after posting my prayers on social media, I found that they resonated with people across denominational and political lines. They gave voice, it seemed, to things many Christians believed God would never be interested in. My hope, of course, was to persuade readers otherwise—that God was, in fact, interested in hearing everything that we have to say to him in prayer.

God cares little about whether we get our prayers "right" or whether we tidy up our lives prior to making our intercessions known. True piety, as the psalmists repeatedly suggest, ought not to be a precondition for talking to God. Showing up is all that's needed, as well as a commitment to being brutally honest with God—honest about our doubts, honest about our anger about unanswered prayers, honest about the failures and fears we might be ashamed to admit out loud, among others.

Stanley Hauerwas puts the point this way in his book of prayers, *Prayers Plainly Spoken*:

> God wants our prayers and the prayers God wants are *our* prayers. We do not need to hide anything from God, which is a good thing given the fact that any attempt to hide from God will not work. God wants us to cry, to shout, to say what we think we understand and what we do not. The way we learn to do all this is by attending to the prayers of those who have gone before.[1]

All aspects of our lives must be prayed, then, lest we become atheists in the quotidian parts of our lives because we have come to believe that these parts are, in fact, godless, devoid of God's interest and care. But that is not the kind of God we encounter in the Psalms, nor in the life and ministry of Jesus, whom the book of Hebrews calls the true Pray-er. He is the infinitely gracious one who eagerly welcomes our whole selves, along with all the details of our lives.

Around the two-year anniversary of the shutdown of our world that Covid-19 demanded of us, I discovered that I had written close to four hundred collect prayers. It was at this

---

[1]Stanley Hauerwas, *Prayers Plainly Spoken* (Downers Grove, IL: InterVarsity Press, 1999), 17.

point that I wondered whether they might become a book of their own. The editors at InterVarsity Press believed that they could, and for that I am deeply grateful.

The Collect Prayer

Three questions that I've often answered over the past few years are: What exactly is a *collect?* Is it a *CAW-lect* or a *cuh-LECT?* (it's the former). And why did I choose to work nearly exclusively with this form of prayer?

To answer the first question, a collect is an old form of prayer, concise in form and immensely useful to any circumstance of life. It is also a theologically disciplined prayer. Dating back to the fifth century, the collect is rooted in a basic biblical pattern that "collects" the prayers of God's people.[2] As C. Frederick Barbee and Paul F. M. Zahl explain:

> This at-first extemporaneous prayer would later also be connected to the Epistle and Gospel appointed for the day. A Collect is a short prayer that asks "for one thing only" . . . and is peculiar to the liturgies of the Western Churches, being unknown in the Churches of the East. It is also a literary form (an art comparable to the sonnet) usually, but not always, consisting of five parts.[3]

---

[2] If you could take a time machine back to churches in fifth-century Rome and were already familiar with the collect, there's a good chance you would recognize the rhythm of the people's intercessions, even if you couldn't understand the Latin of Saint Jerome's world.

[3] C. Frederick Barbee and Paul F. M. Zahl, *The Collects of Thomas Cranmer* (Grand Rapids, MI: Eerdmans, 1999), x.

The five parts that Barbee and Zahl speak of include, nearly always, the following things:

1. Name God.
2. Remember God's activity or attributes.
3. State your petition.
4. State your desired hope.
5. End by naming God again.

While covering a good deal of ground, the collect is notable for its economy. It's a blessedly short prayer. It's short because it typically revolves around one idea only, which in principle is drawn from Scripture. In doing so, several benefits accrue to the one who prays it.

Most basically, it invites us to call to mind what God has done in the past before we make our present petitions known. We remember *before* we request, and we look back on the faithfulness of God in the lives of others *prior* to welcoming the faithfulness of God in our own.

The collect also offers an opportunity to discover how the triune God attends to the details of our lives. If the devil is in the details, as the common saying goes, God is in the details infinitely more so. God is intimately interested in those specific aspects of our lives—doing laundry, suffering illness, aging rapidly, fighting traffic, spending time with a friend— where we find ourselves actually believing, or disbelieving, that God wishes to meet us in the pain and pleasure of our life's circumstances.

Another way of making this point is that the collect is a concrete species of prayer. It deals with one concrete thing without, hopefully, devolving to idiosyncratic vocabulary. My prayer for the pandemic, for instance, was born out of a specific experience that was foisted upon our world, but its language is "open" enough to make it useful to present-day circumstances where plague-like tragedies may require a prayer drawn from the ancient language of the psalmists.

The prayer that I wrote for Phaedra when she makes bone broth (a regular thing in our household) may not feel relevant to 99 percent of humanity. Yet the actual language of the prayer draws attention to ingredients that are, in fact, common to 99 percent of humans on planet earth: root, leaf, fish, fowl, spice, and so on. Surely, I imagine, there will be plenty of occasions to ask God to take the basic elements of creation and to bless them to our health.

The stuff of life, then, that populates collect prayers is of a concrete sort, without being distractingly subjective, and in this way the prayers offer themselves as universally accessible, capable of being prayed by all sorts of people in all manner of life settings.

Yet while I have tried to steer clear of too-subjective language in most of these prayers, it has been impossible to escape the subjective nature of the selection itself.

I am mindful, for instance, of the US-focused nature of the prayers for major holidays and the somewhat random choice of prayers for work. I've written, for example, prayers for Martin Luther King Jr. Day and Juneteenth, but none for Guy Fawkes Night or Chinese New Year. Likewise, I've written prayers for pastors and ministers, but I've included no prayers for accountants or postal workers, though they undoubtedly warrant them.

I've also produced a batch of prayers just for creatives. I've done so not because they deserve our special attention, any more or less than nurses or engineers deserve our attention as performing God-blessed work, but because I've spent a good deal of my life ministering to artists and creatives and I wished to offer to them this particular set of prayers.

All of this, unfortunately, is the nature of an occasionalist book of prayers written by an individual person, rather than a comprehensive one compiled by a denominational task force. My hope, however, is that you will be able to adapt these prayers to serve your own particular needs.

Collects are also typically *written* prayers. Some of us who, like me, were reared in contexts where extemporaneous prayers were privileged over written ones may feel uncomfortable praying such prayers. Yet while it may take a little getting used to, written prayers offer us a unique gift, as I have come to experience firsthand.

In this vein, I've given a good deal of attention to crafting these prayers in the hope that they will reward repeated praying. Much like the poetry of the Psalms, collects involve a dense mix of language and imagery, and the words, at best, say exactly what needs saying to God and what needs saying *continually* to God.[4]

We ought never to tire, for example, of praying the penitential words of Psalm 51 or the exultant but compact language of Psalm 100. The same can be said of the Lord's Prayer. Prayed with a sincere heart, it remains fresh every time.

With the prayer I wrote for those who struggle with mental health, for instance, a good deal of hours were required to get it right. I needed to understand what people in such conditions struggle with, and I needed also to understand which Scriptures might be the right place to camp out, so to speak, for those who would return to this prayer again and again because they find that it gives voice to the yearning of their hearts.

I should also mention, finally, that I am naturally drawn to the musicality of collects. This may be the result of the influence of sixteenth-century Anglican archbishop Thomas Cranmer on my thinking; his prayers "sing" rather than plod along. So while I am not a poet, I have always loved the way words can sound, and I have attempted to retain the sonorous qualities of the English language in these prayers.

A Family of Prayers

I readily admit here that there isn't anything terribly original in this batch of prayers. In fact, there is a good chance readers

---

[4]I write about the distinctive powers of poetry in my book, W. David O. Taylor, *Open and Unafraid: The Psalms as a Guide to Life* (Nashville: Thomas Nelson, 2020).

will hear echoes of others' prayers—the prayers of Saint Paul, or Augustine, or Charles Wesley, along with the wonderfully earthy prayers of the Celts.

While I have tried to infuse fresh language into familiar forms of prayer and to give voice to specifically contemporary situations, I stand in a long tradition of written prayers. I do so not only because humility demands it but also because freshness of language comes not out of rejecting the prayers of our forefathers and mothers but out of a wholehearted immersion in the tradition—in that which has been handed down to us by God's grace.

To be traditional in this sense, as the church historian Jaroslav Pelikan saw it, is to actively receive the "living faith of the dead"[5] as a gift rather than as an imposition. We do not, that is, find our voices as writers in antithetical relation to tradition but *within* and *among* the communion of the saints.

John A. McGuckin, a priest in the Romanian Orthodox Church, writes, "We stand in the presence of the craftsmen and women of the Spirit of God who have gone before us"[6] and to whom we apprentice ourselves in the habit of prayer. The English poet T. S. Eliot says something similar with respect to the work of artists: "No poet, no artist of any art, has his complete meaning alone. His significance, his appreciation is the appreciation of his relation to the dead poets and

---

[5]Jaroslav Pelikan, *The Vindication of Tradition* (New Haven and London: Yale University Press, 1984), 65.
[6]John A. McGuckin, ed. and trans., *Prayer Book of the Early Christians* (Brewster, MA: Paraclete, 2011), xiv.

artists."[7] As far back as the book of Psalms, then, God's people have found immense benefit in writing out their prayers.

This isn't to say that there is no place for spontaneous cries of the heart. While certain ecclesial cultures may feel particularly allergic for liturgical or theological reasons to such extemporaneous practices, I've been blessed over the years to participate in communities that have prayed beautiful prayers "of the moment." There is a certain art to spontaneous prayer that comes, much like the learning of a musical instrument, only with repeated practice.

But for the purposes of this book, I gladly stand on the shoulders of those who have gone before me in the art of the written prayer. I think here of the prayers of the Cappadocian bishop Basil the Great (ca. 330–379), the German monk Thomas à Kempis (1380–1471), and the Spanish Carmelite nun Teresa of Ávila (1515–1582). I think also of the prayer-hymns of Ephrem the Syrian (ca. 306–373).

The Protestant Reformers have likewise inspired me with their crafted prayers, including Martin Luther (1483–1546) and Thomas Cranmer (1489–1556), who spent his greatest energies editing and translating the collects that belonged to the medieval *sacramentaries*, or liturgical books. These contained the prayers of the fifth- and sixth-century Roman church, the three most famous being those attributed to popes Leo I, Gelasius, and Gregory the Great.

---

[7] T. S. Eliot, "Tradition and the Individual Talent," in *Selected Essays: New Edition* (New York: Harcourt Brace, 1932), 4.

I've similarly appreciated the prayers of writers closer in time to myself, such as those of the Anglo-Catholic author Evelyn Underhill (1875–1941) and the Catholic writer Flannery O'Connor (1925–1964), who, as a twenty-one-year-old student at the Iowa Writers' Workshop, kept a record of her prayers in a journal that was eventually published in the 2013 book *A Prayer Journal.*

In more recent history, a small explosion of prayer books has occurred. This includes David Adam's *The Rhythm of Life: Celtic Daily Prayer,* Kate Bowler and Jessica Richie's *The Lives We Actually Have,* and Douglas McKelvey's three volumes of liturgies, *Every Moment Holy.* McKelvey's work in particular has trailblazed a practice of liturgical writing for many today. And I've found much encouragement from the prayers of Cole Arthur Riley's *Black Liturgies: Prayers, Poems and Meditations for Staying Human,* which originally appeared on Instagram.

What makes *Prayers for the Pilgrimage* unique, then? While there is an obvious overlap with the collects that appear in The Book of Common Prayer, this collection of prayers aims at a more contemporary vernacular, less formal or "churchy," as it were, and seeks to address a greater range of concerns for our modern world.

And rather than being liturgies (as with Kayla Craig's *To Light Their Way: A Collection of Prayers and Liturgies for Parents*), freeform prayers (such as the Cláudio Carvalhaes-edited *Liturgies from Below*), or prayer-poems (like Malcolm

Guite's marvelous *Sounding the Seasons*), my book restricts itself largely to the collect form of prayer.

The exception is my inclusion of a small number of prayers that break the collect form, a handful of Celtic prayers, and the prayers I have written for children that attempt to capture the typically musical character of such prayers, which, in the words of the historian William Bright in his 1857 collection of prayers, "the child's ear so readily welcomes."[8]

Lastly, like the Scottish pastor and theologian John Baillie's 1936 book *A Diary of Private Prayer,* my collection seeks to express the heart's deepest yearnings while going beyond the usual territory of so-called spiritual matters in order to show how the ordinary things of our lives are pray-able rather than disposable.

What also makes it unique, of course, is the series of watercolor paintings that accompanies each section of prayers, about which Phaedra writes in the artist statement following this introduction.

A Few Practical Notes

A few practical matters might be useful to note here. First, certain prayers, such as "For When Things Don't Go According to Plan," could just as easily have been placed in a different section. If readers wish to pray such prayers on

[8]William Bright, *Ancient Collects and Other Prayers for the Use of Clergy and Laity* (London: John Henry and James Parker, 1857), vi.

different occasions, they should feel free to do so. Readers should also feel free to change the point of view of these prayers from first person singular ("I ask") to first person plural ("We ask"), and vice versa, as suits the need of the moment.

There are likewise prayers, such as the ones that I have written for the Feast of the Holy Name and the Feast of the Circumcision of Christ, which have been shifted to different days on the church calendar. While usually celebrated on the same day, the eighth day after Christmas, January 1, I have placed these two feasts on separate days in order to give them each their own prayer. I've also written a prayer for New Year's Day, which simply means that a whole host of things can be prayed on this new day of the Gregorian calendar, if one so wishes. The same holds for other prayers like them.

Readers will notice soon enough that I nearly universally begin my prayers with the same address: "O Lord." I've done this partly to retain a measure of rhetorical consistency across the prayers. I could have just as easily, of course, begun my prayers with "O God" or, as I do in certain cases, by addressing them to one of the Divine Persons. I've chosen to use the language of "Lord," however, because it represents a primary way that both Israel and the church address God: in the Hebrew, as *Adonai* or *Yahweh*; in the Greek, as *Kyrios*.

For many, this may make intuitive sense with the Father and the Son, but, as the church has recognized in its ecumenical creeds, the Third Person of the Trinity is equally worthy of being addressed as Lord. In the Nicene Creed, we not only confess our faith in the Holy Spirit, who is "the Lord and giver of Life," but also declare that the Spirit is worthy to be "worshiped and glorified." It's for this reason, then, that I have addressed my Pentecost prayers, for instance, directly to the Spirit.

For those who worship in high-church liturgical settings, three things about these collects will look different: I have consistently used the phrasing "you who," I have made explicit the personal agency of the pray-er by using either "I pray" or "We pray," and I have concluded each prayer by drawing attention to a specific aspect of the character and work of God rather than in the usual christological or trinitarian fashion.

The reasons for such changes are simply this: I see this book less as a direct companion to the church's corporate worship and more as an auxiliary to it. My primary purpose is to support the devotional lives of Christians in order to invite them into a fresh encounter with God, and it's for this reason that my prayers do not strictly adhere to the form one might find in official Anglican, Lutheran, or Catholic prayer books. I would be perfectly happy, though, if readers wished to amend my prayers in order to conform them to the typical pattern of the collect so they might be put to use in a liturgical context.

Our Hope for This Book

What is our hope for this book? Our hope is that readers might find something truly helpful in these prayers, and

Phaedra and I imagine all sorts of readers who may derive benefit from them.

For those who feel that their prayer lives have dried up, our hope is that they will discover in these pages fresh language to revitalize their prayer lives. For those who seek help with praying through the common aspects of their lives—when grumpy or happy, after nightmares, or for tasks that seem impossible, like facing the onset of dementia or the possibility of an irreparable marriage—we trust that they will find plenty of practical assistance for such matters.

For those who find themselves at the margins of the church or, worse, on the brink of losing their faith, our sincerest hope is that they will find here language that lets them give honest expression to the hard edges of their personal lives, as with, say, a struggle with a mental disorder, or to the damaged aspects of their common lives today, such as the warmongering of politicians or the abusive behavior of church leaders.

Our book, then, is not only for those who feel an ardent hunger for God, for whom we pray that this book will serve only to increase their spiritual hungers. Our book is also for those who have lost the will to pray yet wish it were otherwise.

It is for those who worry or wonder whether God has abandoned the world that he so loves in all its minutiae and mundanity, and for those who wish to be found again *by* God in order to find their voice *before* God. The Scottish biblical scholar William Barclay wrote, "Prayer should be such that now and again some will say, 'This means me.'"[9] What Barclay described as a hope for his 1959 book of prayers we hope for much the same with our own.

To all such readers, then, we offer these prayers and paintings in the hope that they will enliven and inspire your own prayers, which the seventeenth-century poet and pastor George Herbert described as "the soul in paraphrase, heart in pilgrimage."[10]

May these prayers help you to open up your heart to God anew and strengthen your bonds of affection with fellow pilgrims who earnestly wish for the same. And may you find joy afresh in your life of prayer with the God who meets you in the face of Jesus Christ and whose Spirit lovingly guides and guards you on the pilgrim way (Psalm 84:5).

* * *

O Lord, you who are the Way of Life, may we walk in your ways this day, we pray, looking to the signposts of your word for guidance and receiving the encouragement of the saints of old for sustenance, so that the demanding, narrow road might become the beloved pilgrim way of our lives. We pray this in the name of the One who walks with us on the way, Jesus Christ himself. Amen.

---

[9]William Barclay, *A Barclay Prayer Book* (Louisville, KY: Westminster John Knox, 2003), 6.

[10]George Herbert, "Prayer (I)," 1633, Poetry Foundation, www.poetryfoundation .org/poems/44371/prayer-i.

PRAYERS FOR LIFE: ARTIST STATEMENT

PHAEDRA TAYLOR

When the pandemic hit, my children were in preschool and third grade. It was already a struggle to maintain a creative practice when they were away for some of the day, but when our preschool shut down and our daughter's schooling turned virtual, my time for making art became almost non-existent.

We were luckier than most. David was already working virtually from home, and my creative work was flexible and could be easily put on hold. I thought I'd just set it aside for a time as we all tried to adjust to what felt like a new normal every week. I found, however, that I struggled emotionally and mentally without the time that I had previously spent, usually deep in contemplative mode, in my studio.

Prayer is inextricably linked to my art practice, and in a world that felt so unpredictable and unmanageable, I needed that time more than ever.

As an experiment, I began making tiny landscapes that I could quickly drop in and out of. One moment I could tear down watercolor paper into small rectangles; in another I could tape down a few pieces. That might be all I could manage for a day, but the next day I might be able to grab five minutes to place some quick brush strokes on my paper. A second layer of color would follow—and then a few moments of drawing in a few finishing touches and I could start another one.

I painted places I longed for, landscapes that were quiet and expansive. In a time when we didn't know if it was even safe to go outside, I needed to spend some time in a wild, free space for a while.

In time, these paintings also became my prayers. By working quickly in between washing hands, laundering masks, cooking, checking infection rates in our state, tidying, monitoring spelling tests, and soothing anxious hearts, I could add a dash of viridian green and cry out: "Lord, help!" I could scribble a horizon line and say: "Jesus, steady me." I could watch the watercolor float on wet paper and plead: "Spirit, give me patience." I could tear paper and pray: "Father, help us be brave."

I could walk away from the studio and return to whatever was being required of me, knowing that my prayers were as real and solid as my paintings—a place I could drop into at any moment that would nourish me once again.

What started as a desperate way to give my brain a measure of sanity turned into a steady and daily practice that I kept up even after things began to settle down in our often-turbulent world. As of this writing, I have painted almost two hundred tiny prayer landscapes. The ones included in this book were made in much the same way as those first attempts, except that my dedicated studio hours have returned. Instead of ten minutes, I'm able to soak deeply into a more expansive prayer space and to let these images emerge.

Two new additions began to appear as I made the work for this book. First, you will find small dwellings nestled in some of these paintings. Second, I've added gold line work and shapes into each image. Why have I done this?

On the one hand, I think of prayer as a landscape that we walk through rather than a destination we arrive at. But isn't it comforting to see the glowing light of a safe and warm house across an expanse of open land? Prayer can feel like a wilderness, but I have also experienced moments of comfort and companionship while traveling across its wild spaces. These little houses try to visually offer those moments. Jesus tells us that he dwells with us and that he is indeed a dwelling place himself. When you see these houses, then, I hope you think of Jesus waiting to meet you there as you walk along in prayer.

On the other hand, the gold elements are an attempt to show a link between the seen and the unseen realities of our world. I often make work about the moments where the veil between the spiritual and the physical is thin. I've experienced myself many of those moments in nature, and I love trying to illustrate that invisible connection with the use of gold lines and heavy shapes. The gold bridges the sky and the land, and it lies over the ridge like a heavy blanket. The gold sometimes drips, other times strikes down, often floats through or presses from behind, and even lies underneath the images like a foundation—all the ways I imagine the world of God interwoven with and infused into our physical world.

My hope is that these images are not just an embellishment to the written prayers but aids in your experience of prayer. When the world seems fast and full, perhaps looking at them will open a moment of stillness and beauty that brings you into a deeper and richer understanding of the gift of prayer.

May the peace of Christ be with you as you journey through the wild landscape of prayer.

PRAYERS FOR MORNING AND EVENING

Morning Prayers

O Lord, you who promise daily bread, may I be faithful to all you have entrusted to me this day, no more and no less, I pray, and let me not become anxious over things that I cannot control, so that I may experience the peace of Christ which guards my heart and mind. I pray this in the name of Jesus, the One who is the Author and Finisher of my faith. Amen.

O Lord, you who make new again and again, enliven the thoughts of my mind, revitalize the cells of my body and cause a fresh outburst of praise to surge in my heart, I pray, so that I may taste the Life that is truly life this day. I pray this in the name of Jesus, the One whose Face is like the shining sun. Amen.

O Lord, you who are the Rising Sun, may I hear and heed your words of life this day, I pray, so that my soul might be refreshed, my heart made wise, my mind enlivened, my care of others renewed and my love of you made full

and true. I pray this in the name of Jesus, the One who is
Eternal Life itself. Amen.

O Lord, you who go before us and behind us, be with us
this day, we pray, as we travel to work and to school, to
places of joy and of sorrow, and to places known and
unknown, so that we might know your safeguarding love
and remember always that our lives are in your hands. We
pray this in the name of our Good Shepherd, Jesus Christ
himself. Amen.

O Lord, you who bless both day and night, pour your
steadfast love over me this day, I pray, and let your song be
with me in the night, so that my entire life might become
a prayer to you. I pray this in the name of Jesus, the One
who ever goes before and behind me. Amen.

O Lord, you who are our peace, may I greet in peace all
whom I meet this day, speaking your word of blessing to
each one with feet that have been shod with the gospel of
peace, so that I might become an emissary of the peace of
Christ that heals and restores. I pray this in the name of
the Reconciling One, Jesus Christ himself. Amen.

O Lord, you who crown me with love and mercy, may my
whole body bless you this day—my eyes and my ears, my
hands and my feet, my head and my heart—and may all

that is within me bless your holy name, so that I may be a blessing to all whom I meet on the way this day. I pray this in the name of the One from whom all blessings flow. Amen.

Evening Prayers

O Lord, you who remain sovereign over all the forces of chaos, be my shelter and comfort this night, I pray, as I lay myself to sleep, so that I might rise in the morning rested and restored, certain that you have set my feet on the path of life. I pray this in the name of Yahweh, the God who is my Sanctuary. Amen.

O Lord, you who promise rest to the weary and heavy-laden, I offer to you my weary body, heavy-laden with the cares of this world, and I ask that you would speak your word of peace to it, so that my body might be repaired through the watches of the night and arise in your grace. I pray this in the name of the One who gives strength to the weary. Amen.

O Lord, you who guide me in the hours of the day and guard me through the watches of the night, I entrust to you all that I said and left unsaid this day, all that I did and did not do, all that I wished this day could have been but was not, and I ask that you would grant me your peace, so that

I might trust you in all things. I pray this in the name of the One who holds my life in tender care. Amen.

O Lord, you who keep watch day and night, I entrust to you this night my vulnerable body as it goes to sleep; may I be reminded in my vulnerability that I am not the master of my life but only its steward, so that I might rise in gratitude for all that you have given to me. I pray this in the name of the God who is my Refuge. Amen.

O Lord, you who neither sleep nor slumber, heal my restless heart, I pray, and ease my anxious mind through the hours of the night, so that I might awake to a new day replenished in body and soul. I pray this in the name of my Guardian Shepherd, Jesus Christ himself. Amen.

O Lord, you who give sleep to your beloved, I entrust to your care this night my weary and wounded body and I ask that you would give me the gift of deep and dreamless sleep, so that I might awake refreshed and ready to do the good work of a new day. I pray this in the name of the God who shields and shelters me. Amen.

PRAYERS FOR MONDAY TO SUNDAY

In the following batch of prayers, I take the divine figures of Norse and Roman mythology, from which we derive our English names for the weekdays, as "types" of Christ in strange garb. The gods of love ("Frigg's Day") and thunder ("Thor's Day"), for example, are no gods at all but only shadows and echoes of the one true God, the God who is love incarnate and whose glory thunders over the waters. I've also written two extra prayers for *sábado* and *domingo*, the terms for Saturday and Sunday in Spanish (as also in the Romance languages more broadly), which draw explicitly from the biblical accounts of worship on the Sabbath and on the day of the Lord.

For Monday ("Moon Day")

O Lord, you who made the moon both to mark the seasons and to rule the night, rule in our hearts this day, we pray, and bless our Monday's work, so that with the moon and the stars we might joyfully praise you at day's end. We pray this in the name of the Maker of heaven and earth, the One who makes the smaller light to rule the night. Amen.

For Tuesday ("Tiw's Day")

O Lord, you who are the God of Angel Armies, defend us, we pray, against all sinister forces that would seek to steal, kill, and destroy the signs of your goodness in our lives, so that we might stand strong and secure in your gracious purposes for us this day. We pray this in the name of the King of kings, Jesus Christ himself. Amen.

For Wednesday ("Woden's Day")

O Lord, you who make a wildly wonderful world, spark our curiosity this day, we pray, dazzle our minds, enkindle our imaginations, and increase in us a childlike sense of wonder, so that we may never grow dull in our study of your world but always be joyfully keen and curious in your creation. We pray this in the name of the Creator of heaven and earth. Amen.

For Thursday ("Thor's Day")

O Lord, you who reveal your glory in the thunder, speak your thunderous word this day, mighty and majestic, we pray, so that we might experience your sovereign protection against all evil powers that would seek to trample or to crush us under. We pray this in the name of the God of glory whose voice thunders across the waters. Amen.

For Friday ("Frigg's Day")

O Lord, you whose love chases after us all the days of our lives, may we live as your beloved this day, we pray, secure and confident in your care for us, so that we might give ourselves away to those who dearly need to see and to sense your love for them in all the cares and occupations of their lives. We pray this in the name of Jesus, the Beloved Son. Amen.

For Saturday 1 ("Saturn's Day")

O Lord, you who are bountiful and generous, help us, we pray, to live in your economy of abundance this day, so that we might become signs of your generative life to all who may be crippled or crushed under by an economy of scarcity, where nothing and no one is good enough. We pray this in the name of Jesus, the One who makes more than enough. Amen.

For Saturday 2 ("sábado")

O Lord, you who rested on the Sabbath in order to delight in your creation, may we live this day, we pray, as a day of grace in contented rest, festive play, generous hospitality, and leisurely relationship, so that we might live every day with a keen sense that, in Jesus, there is always enough. We pray this in the name of Jesus, the One who is our Sabbath Rest. Amen.

For Sunday 1 ("Sun's Day")

O Lord, you whose beauty is radiant like the sun, may we be filled with you wholly this day, we pray, as we praise

your name from the rising of the sun to its setting so that
we might be a radiant reflection of your beauty to all whom
we meet on the way. We pray this in the name of the God
who is our Sun and Shield. Amen.

For Sunday 2 ("domingo")

O Lord, you who are the sovereign ruler of all things in
heaven and on earth and under the earth, may we dwell
this day, we pray, under the shelter of the Most High, so
that we may be wholly at rest in all things, secure in your
providential care over all the details of our lives. We pray
this in the name of Jesus, the One who is the Lord of
lords. Amen.

PRAYERS FOR THE SECULAR CALENDAR

For New Year's Day

O Lord, you who make all things new, I consecrate myself to you on this new day of a new year and I ask that you would grant me the gift of a new song, so that by your Spirit I might sing myself into the reality of Christ's ever-renewing life in this new year to come. I pray this in the name of the One who makes a new heaven and a new earth. Amen.

For the Feast of Saint Valentine

O Lord, you who are the lover of our souls, where my heart is cold for you, kindle it anew with a flame of pure love, I pray, and where my heart is warm, cause my innermost being to burn for you, so that with Saint Valentine I might unashamedly love you in both life and death. I pray this in the name of the Beloved One, Jesus Christ himself. Amen.

For a Lonely Valentine's Day

O Lord, you who have known the bitterness of rejection, I offer to you my fragile heart this day and the painful disappointment of unmet expectations; be with me, I pray, during the lonely hours of this Valentine's Day; and may my loneliness not become oppressive to me but rather an occasion to feel deeply my company with saints throughout the ages who have shared a similar pain, so that I may experience you as the One who makes his home with the lonely hearts. I pray this in the name of Jesus, the One who was abandoned but never abandoned his own. Amen.

For MLK Jr. Day (For the Dignity of All People)

O Lord, you who purchased for God a people from every tribe, tongue, people, and nation, may Dr. Martin Luther King Jr.'s vision for our country be made manifest in the body of Christ, we pray, where the dignity and equality of every person is cherished and where justice and righteousness mark all our dealings with one another, both in word and in deed, so that we might reflect on earth that which is gloriously true in heaven. We pray this in the name of the Lamb who sits upon the throne, Jesus Christ himself. Amen.

For MLK Jr. Day (For Being a People of Peace)

O Lord, you who refused to use the violence of the world to achieve peace, strengthen us, we pray, to be a people of nonviolence in the spirit of your servant Dr. Martin Luther King Jr., rejecting the hostile ways of Herod and all Petrine instincts for violent retribution, so that we might be empowered to do the work of your peaceable kingdom this day. We pray this by the power of your own Spirit. Amen.

For Memorial Day

O Lord, you who make wars cease to the end of the earth, we pray today for the men and women in our armed forces at home and abroad, that you would guard them from all harm, preserve them in the knowledge of your watchcare, and secure in them a peace that surpasses all understanding, so they might be instruments of your peace and justice in the world, in hopeful anticipation of the day when swords shall be beaten into plowshares, spears into pruning hooks, and nation shall not lift up sword against nation, and neither shall they learn war anymore. We pray this in the name of the Prince of Peace, Jesus Christ himself. Amen.

For Mother's Day

O Lord, you who comfort us as a mother comforts her child, grant me your tender care and your fierce protection, I pray, so that I might be reassured of your motherly affections and your visceral love for me this day. I pray this in the name of the One who gathers us under his sheltering wings. Amen.

For Father's Day

O Lord, you who are a father to the fatherless, let your Spirit cause my heart to cry out "Abba, Father!" this day, I pray, so that I might sense your fatherly affections and your paternal care for me in all that I say and do. I pray this in the name of Jesus, the One who shows me fully the face of my Father who is in heaven. Amen.

For Juneteenth

O Lord, you who set the oppressed free, increase in us a love of justice this day, we pray, that we might love it as you love it, upholding the cause of the poor, defending the weak, rescuing the needy, and speaking out for the oppressed, no matter what the cost, so that we might gladly fulfill the law of love. We pray this in the liberating name of Jesus. Amen.

For Independence Day

O Lord, you whose kingdom is not of this world, strengthen our allegiance to your kingdom, we pray, deepen our loyalties to your global body and increase in us our longing for a better country, so that in Jesus' name we might love our nation and our neighbors as pilgrims in a strange land. We pray this in the name of Jesus, the One who truly sets us free. Amen.

For Halloween (For Joy and Festivity)

O Lord, you who clothe us with joy and attire the wildflowers with beauty, may we revel this day in the joy of creativity and in the beauty of merrymaking, we pray, so that we might taste the sweetness of true festivity and delight in the gratuitous abundance of your creation. We pray this in the name of the God who is our True Dresser. Amen.

For Halloween (For the Defeat of all Evils)

O Lord, you who have conquered death and vanquished evil, may we not fear the terror of night nor the plague that stalks by dark, we pray, but rather trust in your power to conquer every cruel and merciless force that seeks to demean and to distort your good creation, so that we might arise this day in the strength of heaven and in the light of the sun. We pray this in the strong name of the Father, the Son, and the Holy Spirit. Amen.

For the Thanksgiving of Good Things

O Lord, you who are the Author of all good things, help us, we pray, to be truly thankful for the good things in our lives—for honest work and a roof over our head, for the bounty of creation, the provision of food, the health of mind and body, the things of beauty that mark our lives, the kindness of neighbors and the love of family and friends—so that in our enjoyment of your generosity we might be equally generous to our neighbor in need, whether they be a friend or a stranger. We pray this in your good name. Amen.

For the Thanksgiving of Hard Things

O Lord, you who are the Author of all good things, help us, we pray, to be truly thankful for the afflictions and hardships that mark our lives, especially for those things that bring to light our weaknesses of character, our limitations of body, our true need of each other, and our great need of you, so that we might witness the power of your Spirit making us by grace a little more like Christ himself. We pray this in the name of the One whose grace is made perfect in weakness. Amen.

For Christmas Eve

O Lord, you who assumed flesh and bone, we praise you this night for your incarnation and for making manifest thereby Love Divine, all loves excelling; make your love incarnate in us, we pray, so that we may become wholly flesh of your flesh and bone of your bone in all that we do and say this day and forever more. We pray this in the name of Jesus, the One whose infant hands shall burst our bands. Amen.

For Sanity on Christmas Eve for Frazzled Parents

O Lord, you who endured the bickering of your disciples, grant me, I pray, this one Christmas miracle: that my children would not bicker with each other from dawn to dusk like rabid animals, so that I do not lose my marbles, shatter my nerves, or fast-track to all gray hairs. I pray this in the name of the One who will help me not die if I hear my children yelling one more time. Amen.

For New Year's Eve (For a Good Ending)

O Lord, you who restore to us the year that the locusts have eaten, we rejoice this day with those who rejoice: for the babies born, the projects completed, the science discovered, the creativity unleashed, the bonds of friendship deepened, and the acts of sacrificial love shared, and we ask that you would decree goodness in our lives beyond that which we could ask or imagine, so that a fresh song of praise might fill our hearts in the year to come. We pray this in the name of Jesus, Goodness himself. Amen.

For New Year's Eve (For a Hard Ending)

O Lord, you who bring all our endings to a good end, we end this year by grieving with those who grieve: for the year that the locusts have eaten, with all its irreparable losses, its traumatic memories, its unfair outcomes, and its many deaths, and we ask that you would console them with your healing presence, so that they might not be afraid or alone in their hour of need. We pray this in the name of the God whose comfort restores us. Amen.

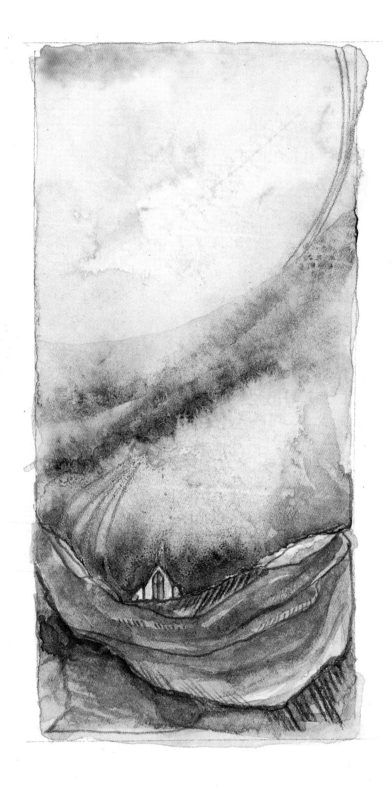

PRAYERS FOR THE CHURCH CALENDAR

Prayers for Advent

Prayers of Light

O Christ, you who are the light of the world, may we live as children of the light this day, we pray, so that we might become emissaries of all that is right and true in your kingdom. We pray this in the name of the One who spoke light into being and it was so. Amen.

O Christ, you who are the light of the world, may your light shine brightly through our lives this day, we pray, so that all whom we meet may be prompted to open up their hearts to our generous Father in heaven. We pray this in the name of the One who causes the light of the righteous to shine brightly. Amen.

O Christ, you who are the light of the world, place our secret sins in the light of your presence this day, we pray, so that we might be freed from their corrosive effects and, in being so freed, raise a joyful song of deliverance in our hearts to you. We pray this in the name of the One who strengthens us according to his word. Amen.

O Christ, you who are the light of the world, be a light in our darkened hearts and minds, we pray, so that we might see and love the truth that would set us free from our addictions to things that grow in the shadow of sin. We pray this in the name of the One who enlightens the eyes of our hearts. Amen.

O Christ, you who are the light of the world, keep us, we pray, from being fearful children of the darkness on account of our continued hate of members of your family and make us instead children of the light who love our brother and sister with the fearless love of Christ, so that we might bear the fruit of righteousness in all that we say and do this day. We pray this in the name of the Son of David, Jesus Christ himself. Amen.

Prayers of Hope

O Lord, you who are the God-Come-Near, strengthen my heart, I pray, to wait in hope for your promises to be fulfilled in my life, so that I might not lose sight of your goodness and create empty golden calves that promise to satisfy my heart's desires but that betray me to my false self and make me sick of soul. I pray this in the name of the One who is never late. Amen.

O Lord, you who feel compassion for the fainthearted, I confess that my heart is neither strong nor brave this day, and I ask that you would carry me in this time of waiting, so that I might know that I am not alone but rather in the strong hands of my Good Shepherd. I pray this in the name of Jesus, the One who leaves the ninety-nine in order to find the one. Amen.

O Lord, you who tell us to keep watch for your coming, open my eyes and ears, I pray, to see and to hear what I cannot see or hear on my own—signs of your gracious presence all around me—so that I might not remain blind or deaf to the evidence of your tangible care for me this day. I pray this in the name of Jesus, the One who made breakfast for his disciples. Amen.

O Lord, you who tell us that in quietness and trust is our strength, help my soul, I pray, to be like quiet waters in the face of the noise of this day and to trust you in the face of all that might cause my faith to waver, so that my heart might be strengthened to wait for your coming in fullness. I pray this in the name of the One who is gentle of heart. Amen.

O Lord, you who are the God-Come-Near, have mercy, I pray, upon my restless need to distract myself today, meet me in the darkness of my small despairs and speak a word of hope to my fearful heart, so that I might wait expectantly for you throughout the hours of this day. I pray this in the name of the One who renews me in my hour of need. Amen.

Prayers of Joy

O Lord, you who have not created us so that we should merely endure existence but that we might delight in the wonder and variety of creation, cause our senses to come alive and alert to your presence in nature, we pray, so that we might savor and steward this world that you so love. We pray this in the name of the One who makes trees that are good for food and pleasing to the sight. Amen.

O Lord, you who are the God of joy unspeakable, turn my tears, I pray, into songs of laughter and make my wilderness blossom with life this day, so that with the morning stars I might sing for gladness without holding anything back. I pray this in the name of Jesus, the One who endured all things for the joy set before him. Amen.

O Lord, you who are merciful and kind, protect us this day, we pray, from the sorrows of life that would rob our hearts of joy, so that our hearts may remain open to you in glad obedience and turned outward toward our neighbor in warm affection. We pray this in the name of the One who guards our hearts from turning fearful. Amen.

O Lord, you whose joy does not deny the affliction of the cross but instead penetrates death and hell, send your joy into the affliction of our own lives, we pray, that it may find and restore us in our distress, so that we may be a people of irrepressible joy and infectious laughter to all whom we meet this day. We pray this in the name of the One whose joy is everlasting. Amen.

O Lord, you whose resurrection is like a laugh freed forever, grant us the grace this day, we pray, to become a people of resilient joy, so that with the morning stars we might sing your praise and with the festive throng we might come to your house with shouts of hallelujah. We pray this in the name of our Bright Morning Star. Amen.

Prayers of Trust

O Lord, you who did the impossible for Elizabeth and Zechariah, protect our hearts, we pray, from doubting your word in our own lives, so that we might praise your name when we witness the fulfillment of your promises, no matter how long they may take to be fulfilled. We pray this in the name of the One who remains infinitely gentle with the faint of heart. Amen.

O Lord, you whose word is trustworthy and true, strengthen my heart, I pray, to say with Mary this day, "Let it be to me according to your word," whether in strength or in weakness, in fullness or in emptiness, so that I may behold the fulfillment of your promises in my life. I pray this in the name of the One for whom nothing is impossible. Amen.

O Lord, you who offer your Flesh as life for the whole world, help us, we pray, to open our tired hands and our hungry hearts to you this day in order to receive this imperishable food, so that you might nourish us with your very life while we wait for the fulfillment of your promises in our lives. We pray this in the name of Jesus, the Lamb of God. Amen.

O Lord, you who come to us in the fullness of time, may we not see the days of our waiting as wasted but rather as days in which we are becoming large with the life of God in us, we pray, so that our expectancy might be marked by a resilient hope rather than by an embittered sorrow. We pray this in the name of the One who arrives in the nick of time. Amen.

O Lord, you who establish the work of my hands, go before and behind me, be above and below me, and be also my guide and my guardian, I pray, so that I may trust you in all things and fulfill your good purposes for me this day.

I pray this in the name of the Shepherd of my soul, Jesus
Christ himself. Amen.

For Saint Nicholas Day (December 6)

O Lord, you who defend always the cause of the poor,
place in our hearts a deep and irresistible desire to serve
the poor this day, we pray, so that we may be worthy
to be called by your name and live out the example of
Saint Nicholas in our own time and place. We pray this
in the name of Jesus, the One who became poor for our
sake. Amen.

For Saint Lucia Day (December 13)

O Lord, you who are the Light of Life, inspire us this
day by the example of Saint Lucia so that we, not fearing
persecution or loss of life, might bring your light to those
who find themselves in dark places, so that all might see
and believe that you are the Light who has overcome
the darkness. We pray this in the name of Jesus, the Life-
Light. Amen.

For the Virgin Mary

O Lord, you who throw down the mighty from their
thrones and lift up the humble from the earth, protect
us, we pray, from becoming enthralled by the ways of the
Caesars and the Herods of this world who use their power
to oppress the least and the last, and grant us instead the

heart of a Mary, the God-bearer, so that we might rejoice in
the way of humility and glory in the work of simple service.
We pray this in the name of God our Savior. Amen.

For Saint Joseph

O God, you who graced Joseph to be a father to your Son,
grace us also to be fathers and mothers to the fatherless
and motherless, sons and daughters to the childless,
brothers and sisters and aunts and uncles and grand-
parents to the lonely, so that we might be healing agents
of your familial love this day. We pray this in the name of
Jesus, our Great Brother. Amen.

Prayers for Christmastide

For the First Day of Christmas

O Lord, you who are the God-With-Us, we join all of
creation this day in glad adoration at your birth and we
offer to you our hearts anew, so that your presence may be
richly felt and always welcomed in our lives, this day and
evermore. We pray this in the name of Jesus, the One who
is the Joy of all Creation. Amen.

For the Second Day of Christmas (Saint Stephen's Day, December 26)

O Lord, you who remain faithful to the end, grant us, we
pray, the spirit of Saint Stephen this day, so that we might
bear public witness to your name with a Spirited courage

and a humble heart, fearing neither persecution nor death. We pray this in the name of the Son of Man who stands at the right hand of God, Jesus Christ himself. Amen.

For the Third Day of Christmas (Saint John the Apostle's Day, December 27)

O Lord, you who gladly welcomed the affection of Saint John the Beloved, may we, like him, not be ashamed or embarrassed to show our affections for you in public or in private, so that we might be a people who love you wholly from the heart. We pray this in the name of the Beloved One, Jesus Christ himself. Amen.

For the Fourth Day of Christmas (Feast of the Holy Innocents, December 28)

O Lord, you who weep with Rachel whose children are no more, may we remember this day all the children who have been lost to miscarriage, disease, abuse, neglect, or poverty, so that those who weep for their little ones may not grieve alone but rather in the company of saints who weep with those who weep. We pray this in the name of the God of Jeremiah. Amen.

For the Fifth Day of Christmas

O Lord, you who graced Mary not only to birth the Christ child but also to nurse, to clean, to console, and to change his diapers, may we see the miraculous in the mundane, so that we might experience your extraordinary grace in the ordinary circumstances of our lives. We pray this in the name of the Truly Human One, Jesus Christ himself. Amen.

For the Sixth Day of Christmas

O Lord, you who startled the shepherds with the angelic appearance, startle us, we pray, out of our indifference to the miraculous story of your birth, so that we may never take for granted that the Maker became something Made in order to remake us anew. We pray this in the name of the Eternally Begotten of the Father who began to be in a baby born of Mary. Amen.

For the Seventh Day of Christmas

O Lord, you who refuse to be domesticated by our feasts and fasts, terrify us this day by your awful presence, we pray, so that we, like the shepherds of old, might encounter afresh the awe-filled news of Christ's birth in our own festivities. We pray this in the name of Jesus, the One who sits enthroned between the cherubim and before whom seraphim shield their eyes. Amen.

For the Eighth Day of Christmas (Feast of the Circumcision of Christ, January 1)

O Lord, you who were circumcised on the eighth day, help us to remember, we pray, that neither circumcision nor uncircumcision means anything, but only new creation because we have been marked by your death and resurrection, so that we might live as emblems of your new creation this day. We pray this in the name of Jesus, the Firstborn over all creation. Amen.

For the Ninth Day of Christmas (Feast of the Holy Name)

O Lord, you who were nicknamed by angels and mortals, grant us the grace this day, we pray, to live into our true name, that name that is written on a white stone, so that we might live fully abandoned to you and fully given over to our neighbor in love. We pray this in the name of Jesus, the One whose name is above every name. Amen.

For the Tenth Day of Christmas

O Lord, you who speak a word of comfort to old and young alike, grant us, we pray, a heart of the prophetess Anna who persevered to the end in her devotion to you, so that we, inspired by our elder saints, might bear witness to your faithfulness in our own lives to generations to come. We pray this in the name of the Ancient of Days. Amen.

For the Eleventh Day of Christmas

O Lord, you who speak a word of comfort to old and young alike, grant us, we pray, the spirit of a Simeon so that we too, being filled by the Holy Spirit, might bear witness to your salvation and speak blessing to all whom we meet this day, so that we may remain a faithful witness to your good news all the days of our lives. We pray this in the name of the Glorious One. Amen.

For the Twelfth Day of Christmas

O Lord, you whose birth brings peace on earth, perform a miracle in our hearts, we pray, by making us peacemakers with those with whom we can no longer imagine ourselves at peace, nor will ourselves to make peace, so that we might become emissaries of the good news of the incarnation. We pray this in the name of the Prince of Peace, Jesus Christ himself. Amen.

Prayers for Epiphanytide

For the Visit of the Magi

O Lord, you who were manifested to the world at the visit of the Magi, manifest yourself to the world today, we pray, as the king who refuses to use the violence of the world to achieve peace on earth, so that we might be strengthened to do the work of your peaceable kingdom. We pray this in the name of the King of kings, Jesus Christ himself. Amen.

For Growing in Wisdom

O Lord, you who grew in wisdom, may the grace of God be upon us in all that we do this day, we pray, so that we might be wise in how we live, whether in success or in failure, in strength or in weakness, in plenty or in want. We pray this in the name of Jesus, the One in whom are hidden all the treasures of wisdom. Amen.

For the Flight to Egypt

O Lord, you who escaped to Egypt in order to flee Herod's violence, be with us, we pray, in our own proximity to harm and help us to trust not only the care of your holy family but also the care of your mighty arm, so that we may discover you as the refuge of our body and soul. We pray this in the name of the One who hides us in the shadow of his wings. Amen.

For the Feast of the Baptism of Our Lord (January 8)

O Lord, you who received the benediction of your Father at your baptism, may we live into our baptismal identity this day, we pray, so that we may rest assured that, prior to having accomplished anything or made something of our lives or acquired a name for ourselves, we are called your beloved. We pray this by the Spirit who floods our hearts with the love of God. Amen.

For Shrove Tuesday

O Lord, you who promise to us the "fat of the land" and save the best wine for last, we thank you for your generous provision in our lives and we ask that you would help us

to live within your economy of abundance this day, so that
we might be generous in word and in deed to all whom
we meet. We pray this in the name of the One who makes
more than enough. Amen.

Prayers for Lent

For Ash Wednesday

O Lord, you who invite us to die to ourselves so that we
might find ourselves anew, help me, I pray, not to be too
full of to-do lists and deadlines and wants and shoulds
during this season of Lent, so that there is no space for you
to do your work of transformation in me, but grant me, I
pray, the grace to welcome your Spirit's work to mortify my
flesh, so that I might fully participate in Christ's sufferings
and know the power of his resurrection during this forty-
day pilgrimage. I pray this in the name of Jesus, the One
who heals us by his wounds. Amen.

For the First Sunday of Lent

O Lord, you who discipline those whom you love, grant me
a special grace this Lent, I pray, to embrace the disciplines
that would enable me to love you with all of my body, so
that my body might be freed from the passions that draw
me away from you and be filled with the passions that
draw me near in order that I might more readily fulfill your
good purposes for me as your disciple. I pray this in the
name of Jesus, the One who calls me his own. Amen.

For the Second Sunday of Lent

O Lord, you who are neither ashamed nor surprised by our
neediness, we offer to you this day our needy bodies, hearts,
and minds, and ask that you would speak your healing
word to our bodies, your comforting word to our hearts,
and your word of peace to our minds, so that we might
experience your provision of grace in our hour of need. We
pray this in the name of the One who sees us fully. Amen.

For the Third Sunday of Lent

O Lord, you who daily bear our burdens, strengthen
our hands and expand our heart's capacity to bear one
another's burdens, we pray, so that we might offer your
generous care to friend and neighbor alike who may feel
crushed under by the trials and troubles of their lives. We
pray this in the name of Jesus, the One whose burden is
light. Amen.

For the Fourth Sunday of Lent

O Lord, you who are mighty to save, grant me, I pray,
pardon from all past sins, courage to resist all present temptations, and protection against all evils to come, so that I
might taste the victory of your life-giving power this day
and commend your saving grace to others who face their
own troubles and temptations. I pray this in the name of
Jesus our Redeemer. Amen.

For the Fifth Sunday of Lent

O Lord, you who fasted in the wilderness in order to leave us an example that we should follow, grant, I pray, that the mortification of my body might result in the nourishment of my soul and that the sanctification of my soul might result in a body that is readily disposed to your service this day, so that I might be unreservedly yours, body and soul. I pray this in the name of Jesus, the One who meets me with love in the wilderness. Amen.

For Palm Sunday

O Lord, you who were cheered and jeered by the very same crowd, have mercy, I pray, upon my own duplicitous ways—confessing one sin openly while hiding another, blessing you out of one side of my mouth while cursing my neighbor out of the other, smiling in public but raging in private, lauding justice but denying it in practice, loving God and money equally—so that I may be this day a person of integrity, being one thing truly, through and through, no matter what the cost. I pray this in the name of Jesus, the One who has loved me to the end. Amen.

Note: While the following prayers belong properly to the Stations of the Cross liturgy, I have assigned them instead to specific days of Holy Week.

For Holy Monday

O Lord, you who repeatedly suffered the selfish impositions of others, grant us the humility of Simon of Cyrene, who carried a cross that was not his own and who discovered a Savior that he did not expect; grant us this humility, we pray, in the face of every temptation to become indifferent to others' burdens or to resent the need to carry a burden that is not our own, so that we might see you in every act of service that we perform on behalf of a stranger. We pray this in the name of Jesus, the One who came to serve and not to be served. Amen.

For Holy Tuesday

O Lord, you who met your mother on the way to the cross but could not prevent the sword from piercing her heart, grant us, we pray, the comfort of your Holy Spirit and the consolation of friends when we too feel abandoned or unloved in any way, so that we may never be alone in our griefs. We pray this in the name of Jesus, our Sympathetic Priest. Amen.

For Holy Wednesday

O Lord, you who were not embarrassed to weep in public, may we, like the women of Jerusalem, weep with sorrow at the sight of your suffering and not be ashamed to weep for our own sin that required your sacrifice on the cross, so

that we might be wholehearted in our love for you this day.
We pray this in the name of Jesus, the One who keeps all
our tears. Amen.

For Maundy Thursday

O Lord, you who took up the towel in order to leave us
an example that we should follow, inspire in us this day
a desire, we pray, to serve and to discover the freedom of
serving without notice or recompense, so that we may experience the joyful satisfaction of serving our neighbor for
your sake. We pray this in the name of Jesus, the One who
is the servant of all. Amen.

For Good Friday

O Lord, you who let your body be taken, broken, and
given away for the life of the world, take our own bodies,
we pray, broken by sickness, sorrow, shame, or age, and
bless them, so that they might become agents of your
healing in our broken world this day. We pray this in the
name of Jesus, our bruised and battered Savior. Amen.

For Holy Saturday

O Lord, you who sojourned in the in-between-ness of Holy
Saturday, grant us the grace, we pray, to remain faithful
to you between this dark time of our own Holy Fridays
and the light of our yet-to-come Holy Sundays, so that we

might not lose hope during these long hours of waiting. We pray this in the name of Jesus, the One who keeps watch with us. Amen.

Prayers for Eastertide

For the First Sunday of Eastertide

Resurrected Lord, you whom death could not conquer, make dry bones live, awaken deadened minds, revive barren hearts, restore broken relations, and make streams appear in the wastelands of our lives, we pray, so that we might experience your resurrection power this day and praise you with shouts of joy. We pray this in the name of Jesus, the One who raises us up to new life. Amen.

For the Second Sunday of Eastertide

Resurrected Lord, you who make room in your family for the doubters, the troubled, and the failures, enfold me, I pray, in the care of your body, so that I too might proclaim this day with Saint Thomas, "My Lord and my God!" whether with a feeble or an emboldened faith. I pray this in the name of Jesus, the One who in love extends to me his pierced hands. Amen.

For the Third Sunday of Eastertide

Resurrected Lord, you who command us to preach the gospel to all of creation, may we speak your word of blessing this day, we pray, to the birds of the air, the beasts of the field, the fish of the sea, and the creepy-crawlies of the earth, so that all of creation might know and love you wholly. We pray this in the name of the One who created the heavens and the earth. Amen.

For the Fourth Sunday of Eastertide

Resurrected Lord, you who startled the disciples with your resurrected presence, startle us out of our own overfamiliarity with the gospel, we pray, so that the good news of your risen life might become weird and wonderful again to us this day. We pray this in the name of Jesus, the One who walks through walls and disappears from rooms. Amen.

For the Fifth Sunday of Eastertide

Resurrected Lord, you who entrusted the first word of your resurrection to Mary Magdalene, Joanna, Mary the mother of James, Salome, and the other women, may we too believe the word that you have entrusted to the women in our community, so that we might not be rebuked for our unbelief. We pray this in the name of the Son of the God-bearer, Jesus Christ himself. Amen.

For the Sixth Sunday of Eastertide

Resurrected Lord, you who revealed yourself in the breaking of the bread and who delighted to share breakfast with your disciples, may we see you not only in the

Eucharistic meal that we share with your Body but also in our own common meals, so that we might delight in each other's company as you do in ours. We pray this in the name of Jesus, the Bread of Life. Amen.

For the Seventh Sunday of Eastertide

Resurrected Lord, you who opened the eyes of the disciples so that they might recognize your presence with them, open my eyes, I pray, so that I might not be blind to your presence at home, at work, or in my exchanges with friend and stranger alike. I pray this in the name of Jesus, the One who opens the eyes of the blind. Amen.

For Ascension Day (to Be Prayed the Fortieth Day After Easter)

O Lord, you who rise like fire into the heavens, rise in our hearts this day, we pray, so that we might enthrone you here on earth and welcome your rule in all that we do and say this day. We pray this in the name of Jesus, the One who, in leaving the few behind, draws ever nearer to all. Amen.

Prayers for Pentecost

For the Harmony of Christ's Discordant Body

O Spirit of God, you who turned the chaos of Babel into the harmony of Pentecost, take the many discordant parts of Christ's body this day, we pray, and make them one, so that a watching world may see and believe in the One who holds all things together. We pray this in the name of Jesus, the One who ever prays that we might be one. Amen.

For the Fire of God to Become a Fire in Our Bones

O Spirit of God, you who set the disciples aflame with the fire of God, put a fire in our bones, we pray, so that we, in Jesus' name and for his sake, might preach the good news to the poor, heal the brokenhearted, proclaim freedom for the prisoners and recovery of sight to the blind, and set the oppressed free. We pray this in the life-giving name of Jesus. Amen.

Prayers for the End of the Church Year

For Trinity Sunday (to Be Prayed on the Sunday After Pentecost)

O God, you who reveal yourself as a communion of triune love: may the Father bless me and make of me this day what he will; may the Son bind himself to me and make me his own this day; and may the Spirit fill me and bring me to a good end this day, so that the triune life might be made manifest in all that I say and do. I pray this in the name of the Father, the Son, and the Holy Spirit. Amen.

For All Saints' Day (November 1)

O Lord, you who call us saints, fill me afresh, I pray, with the holiness of the Father, increase in me the humility of

Christ, and purify me of all entangling sins by your Spirit, so that I too may be called a saint this day, aflame with the love of God. I pray this in the name of the Father, the Son, and the Holy Spirit. Amen.

For All Souls Day (November 2)
O Lord, you who are the God of the living and the dead, we thank you this day for the cloud of witnesses that surrounds us and we pray that we may be inspired by their example, so that we may not grow weary in the face of suffering or faint in the hour of trial. We pray this in the name of Jesus, the One who is faithful till the end. Amen.

For Christ the King Sunday
O Lord, you whose kingdom is right-side up and upside down, rule in our hearts this day, we pray, so that by your Spirit, your kingdom of justice and mercy, righteousness and love might be joyfully established among us as it is in heaven. We pray this in the name of Jesus, the One whose peaceable kingdom is from everlasting to everlasting. Amen.

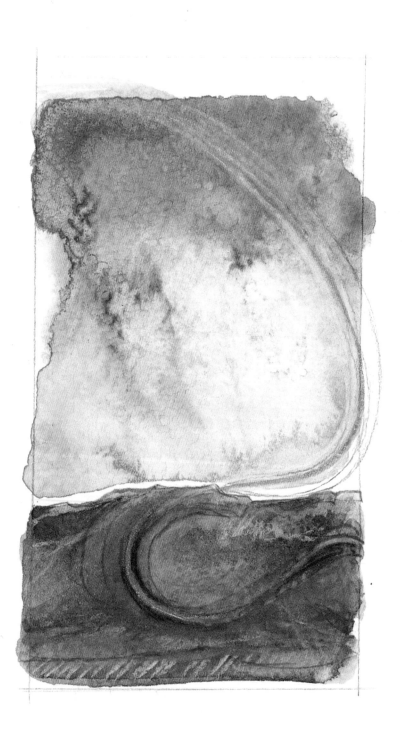

PRAYERS FOR BIRTH TO DEATH

For the Birth of a Child

O Lord, you from whom all blessings flow, we praise you for the safe delivery of this child and we thank you for the beautiful gift of [Name]; with a fullness of heart, we receive [Name] as a grace to our family and ask that you would guide and guard us as we seek to raise [him/her] to know and to love you and to fulfill your good purposes for [him/her]. We pray this in the name of the One who is the Author of all good things. Amen! Amen! Amen!

For One's Own Birthday

O Lord, you who rejoice over me with singing, I thank you for my birthday today and ask that you would bless me, from head to toe and inside out, so that I might burst with life in the year to come and fulfill your good purposes for me all the days of my life. I pray this in the name of the One who exults over me with shouts of joy. Amen.

For Another's Birthday

O Lord, you who formed us in the womb, we pray your blessing on [Name] today as we celebrate [his/her] birthday; may [she/he] know how thoroughly [she/he] is loved, from head to toe and inside out, so that [she/he] might fulfill your good purposes for [her/his] life in the year to come. We pray this in the name of the One who rejoices over us with singing. Amen.

For the Adoption of a Child

O Lord, you who have made us your children by adoption and by grace, we thank you for the arrival of this beautiful child into our family. Our hearts burst with happiness and we marvel at your goodness. We thank you for hearing our cries for mercy and we say, "Blessed be your name!" As we begin this journey with this little one, we pray that you would make us joyful in hope, patient in suffering, and constant in our prayers for [Name], and we entrust [his/her] life into your sovereign care, even as we daily entrust ours to you. May God the Father, who adopted a people in Egypt, always be [Name's] Abba; may God the Son, who himself was adopted, always be [Name's] true brother; and may God the Spirit, who makes us a family, be [Name's] source of peace all the days of [his/her] life, so that God the Holy Trinity may always be [Name's] truest home. We pray this in your good name. Amen.

For the Beginning of a New Season of Life

O Lord, you who began your earthly ministry in God's
good time, bless, we pray, the beginning of this new season
of life: bless the adventures that await us, the newness
that excites us, the strangeness that will surprise us, and
the growth that will be required of us; grant us also your
peace that passes all understanding to guard our hearts
and minds in Christ Jesus, so that we might begin this
new season in faith, hope, and love, trusting that you go
before and behind us in all things. We pray this in the
name of the One who superintends in love all our earthly
sojourns. Amen.

For the Ending of a Season of Life

O Lord, you who ended your earthly ministry in God's
good time, we give you thanks for the ending of this season
of life: for the gifts of grace that nourished us, the experiences of hardship that deepened our character, the happy-
sad moments that we encountered along the way, the
friendships that sustained us, and the memories that we
will cherish for years to come; grant us your peace, we pray,
with all that we leave behind and your joy with all that
awaits us ahead, so that we might end this season in faith,
hope, and love. We pray this in the name of the One who
brings all our stories to a good end. Amen.

For a Midlife Crisis

O Lord, you who are the God of the lost and found, have mercy upon me in this experience of being lost in my own self; quiet my restless heart, I pray, revive my sluggish mind, nurse my weary body, and tame my irritable spirit; rescue me also from both venial and mortal sins that would wound and warp my humanity, and show me the way forward where none appears clearly, so that I may walk with kindred others in the way that you have appointed for me. I pray this in the name of the One who is my Anchor and Refuge. Amen.

For Aging Well

O Lord, you who call our gray hairs a crown of glory, grant me the grace, I pray, to age well: to grieve the loss of vitality in my body, the depletion of strength in my bones, the impotence of immune systems, the increase of wrinkled skin, and the expanse of gray hair; keep me also from an embittered and fearful heart on account of all such vulnerabilities of old age; grant that I may grow childlike of heart, resilient of spirit, rich in friendship, humble of character, and generous of nature, so that I might become a blessing to young and old alike this day. I pray this in the name of the One who blesses the aged with wisdom and fullness of days. Amen.

For an Untimely Death

O Lord, you who wept over the untimely death of your beloved friend Lazarus, we too weep over the untimely death of our beloved one; as their life has been suddenly snatched from us, grasp us, we pray, with your care; as they are now far from us, be near to us this hour; and where we feel empty inside, fill us up with your resurrection life; watch with us, dear Jesus, and watch over us, and be our comfort in the face of all that feels inconsolable, so that we might be those whom you call blessed because they mourn. We pray this in Jesus' name, the Man of Sorrows and the Lamb of God, who makes all things new. Amen.

For Gratitude in the Death of a Beloved One

O Lord, you who wept over the death of your beloved friend Lazarus, we too weep over the death of our beloved one, [Name]; we weep over all that has been lost: their touch, their voice, their presence, what they would have made of the world that you so love, all that they called out in each of us and all the beauty that shone through them; as they are now far from us, be near to us, we pray; be our comfort in this time of grief, even as we seek to be a comfort one to another, so that we might be those whom you call blessed because they mourn. We pray this in the name of the resurrected Christ, our Bright Morning Star. Amen.

For the Fear of Death

O Wounded Christ, you who have gone to the monstrous depths and swallowed death whole, tasting its bitter finality and conquering it once for all, free me, I pray, from the fear of death this day and comfort me in the losses that I experience on account of it, so that my heart might be infused with your resurrecting life and set its hope upon the promise of the new creation. I pray this in the name of the Resurrection and the Life, Jesus Christ himself. Amen.

PRAYERS FOR JOY
AND SORROW

For the Triple Power of Joy

O Lord, you whose coming is a cause for joy to the whole world, may your joy be a strength, we pray, for the tired of body, a holy medicine for the faint of spirit, and a bond of friendship for the estranged, so that your joy might be a taste this day of our true home in the midst of exile. We pray this in the name of Jesus, the One who promises to make our joy complete. Amen.

For a Good Surprise

O Lord, you who are good and kind, I rejoice in the good news that I have received this day and I thank you for surprising me with such bounty and for giving me friends to share in this joy; may I take none of it for granted but savor it deep in my heart, I pray, so that I might never forget that you are good. I pray this in the name of the One who is generous to a fault. Amen.

For the Joyful Life of Jesus

O Lord, you who speak and creatures come into being, breathe new life into existence from that which is dead, I pray, and cause joy to burst into being out of the sorrows of my life, so that I may experience afresh this day the joyous, resurrecting life of Jesus. I pray this in the name of the One whose presence is the fullness of joy. Amen.

After a Great Victory

O Lord, you who are great and mighty, I thank you for this victory, I shout for joy, and I revel in the absolute goodness of it. I say, "Amen!" And I pray that I might not only savor this victory but also be gracious toward those who have not won, so that I might win with humility and celebrate with dignity. I pray this in your good and glorious name. Amen.

After a Hard Defeat

O Lord, you who are close to the brokenhearted, I confess that this defeat has left me feeling both miserable and devastated; hold me, I pray, and help me to see the way forward, so that I might hear the sounds of gladness again and rise up in hope for a new day of good work. I pray this in the name of the Consolation of Israel, Jesus Christ himself. Amen.

For Joy when It Is Hard to Come By

O Lord, you who are the Fount of Joy, may your joy be my strength where I am weak, I pray, and may it be a tonic for the troubles of my soul, so that I may experience the reviving power of your miraculous joy this day. I pray this in the name of the One who makes our joy become like a river that overflows its banks. Amen.

For Feeling Low

O Lord, you who lay me down in the dust of death, may this place of lowliness not have the last word in my life but rather become a place from which something miraculously new is born, so that I might praise you fully and freely in this humble place. I pray this in the name of the One who raises me up from the dust and breathes upon me the life of heaven. Amen.

For a Beleaguered Heart

O Lord, you who promise to hold and to help us in our hour of need, carry my weary body this day, I pray, and care for my beleaguered heart, so that I might not lose hope in these trying and troubling times. I pray this in the name of Jesus, the One who carries all my burdens. Amen.

For Those Who Don't Feel Loved by God

O Lord, you who gather your people like a hen gathers her chicks under her wings, be no longer distant from me, I pray, and leave me no longer in this painful place of exile from your love, but draw me to your tender-loving care and place me under the shelter of your wings, so that I might feel your personal and palpable affections for me this day. I pray this in the name of the One who hears my cry out of the depths. Amen.

For Being Mad at God

O Lord, you who welcome our bitter tears and our raging words of protest, cease your silence and hear me this day: *Awake, Lord! Rouse yourself! Heed my cries! Be the God that you say you are and do not abandon me to my pain!* Show yourself, I pray, and meet me in the depths, so that I may know that there is a God in heaven who hears my voice and sustains me in the hour of my need. I pray this in the name of the God of Job. Amen.

For Parents Whose Children Have Abandoned the Faith

O Lord, you who keep watch with us in the far country, grant me the grace, I pray, to bear the sorrow of my own child who finds himself/herself in the far country; grant me also hope in the face of despair, patience for a heart that is faint, and the ability to remain present to my child even when it feels painful, so that, like the prodigal son's father, I too might keep perpetual watch and retain a heart of compassion for my child whom you, O Christ, love with a fierce and indefatigable love. I pray this in the name of Jesus, the One who is our Cornerstone. Amen.

For Those Suffering from Dementia

O Lord, you who sojourn with us in the shadowlands, be present, we pray, to our beloved one as they drift confusedly about in that disorienting place between memory and oblivion, so that they might experience your enfolding peace and tangible presence this day. We pray this in the name of Jesus, the One who is our True North. Amen.

For Anger

O Lord, you whose holy anger heals, take our burning words, we pray, and protect us from the desire for revenge; by the power of your Spirt keep our anger from turning violent and destructive and make our anger instead a faithful anger, so that it might become fuel for the mending of broken things in our world. We pray this in the name of Jesus, the One whose righteous anger overcomes evil. Amen.

For Sadness

O Lord, you who weep with those who weep and who draw near to the broken in body and in spirit: hear our prayer; do not be deaf to our pain; bring an end to our distress; preserve our lives; rescue us and heal us, we pray, so that we might join the company of those who take refuge in you and praise your holy name. We pray this in the name of Jesus, a Man of Sorrows, acquainted with grief, on whom we cast all our cares. Amen.

For Being Stressed Out (After Saint Basil)

O Lord, you who are the calm harbor of all who are beset by the tempests of this life, calm my anxious mind, I pray, speak your word of peace to my troubled heart and heal my restless body, so that I may come to the end of this day in peace rather than in fear. I pray this in the name of the One who keeps and quiets my soul. Amen.

For God's Ear to Be Inclined to the Hurting

O Lord, you who receive my prayers like rising incense before you, hear me when I cry out to you this day, I pray, so that I might hear your voice speaking a word of comfort and consolation to my wounded heart. I pray this in the name of the Spirit of God who intercedes for me with groanings too deep for words. Amen.

For Tired Hearts

O Lord, you who make and mend the human heart, incline my heart to yourself this hour, I pray; melt and mold it, cure and repair it, fill and form it, so that I might give and receive your love to all whom I meet this day. I pray this in the name of the One who revives the heart after it has seen many troubles and calamities. Amen.

For Losing Out on an Opportunity

O Lord, you who heal the brokenhearted, I offer to you the sharp pain and the deep disappointment at losing out on something I had hoped to have won and I ask that you might reassure me of your good purposes for me, so that I might trust you in all things. I pray this in the name of Jesus, the One Who Never Gives Up on me. Amen.

For Perpetual and Painful Waiting

O Lord, you who at times take centuries to fulfill your promises, grant us the grace this day, we pray, to wait patiently for you to answer our prayers, which we have prayed all these long days and years, and the grace also to remain faithful to you in the meanwhile, so that we might know that we have not been abandoned but are fully enveloped in the care of our Good Shepherd. We pray this in the name of the God of Abraham and Sarah. Amen.

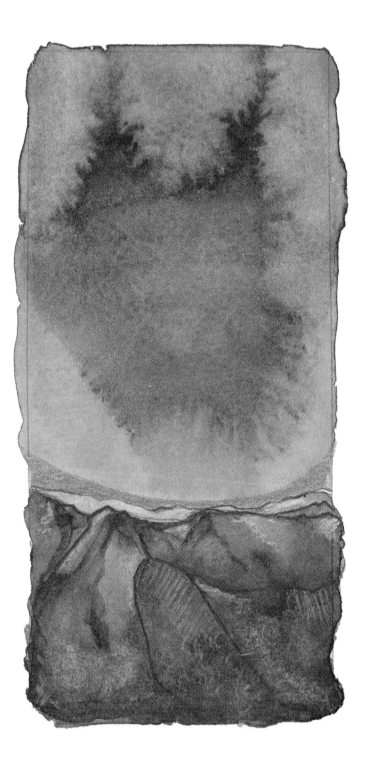

PRAYERS FOR SICKNESS AND HEALING

For the Healing of the Body

O Lord, you who healed the sick and touched the leper,
heal my body, I pray, have mercy upon my soul, console
my weary heart, and sustain me in my hour of need, so that
I might endure this illness with patience and be brought to
full recovery in the joyful certainty that you are my haven
and my health. I pray this in the name of Jesus, my Great
Physician. Amen.

For Those Who Are Chronically Sick or in Pain

O Lord, you who hear and heed the cry of the needy, be a
succor to me in this prolonged hour of trial, I pray, sustain
me when strength of body and heart fail me, and make
things possible in the face of all that seems impossible,
so that I may know you as my true companion in these
trying days and lonely nights. I pray this in the name of my
Healer and Haven. Amen.

For a Child in Need of Healing

O Lord, you who placed your hand upon the children in
order to bless them, heal this child's body, we pray, make
manifest your Spirit's resurrecting power, and sustain these
parents in their hour of need, so that together they might
know you as a haven of protection and a healer of body
and soul. We pray this in your infinitely compassionate
name. Amen.

For the Healing of a Family Member

O Lord, you who are our sun and shield, place your
healing hands, we pray, upon [Name's] body and bless
[him/her] with the comforting presence of your Spirit,
so that [he/she] might rest in your tender care this day;
we pray also for the rest of the family that they might
experience your protective custody and receive heavenly
wisdom and grace in their hour of need. We pray this in
the mighty name of Jesus. Amen.

For Those Who Suffer in Their Bodies

O Lord, you who bear in your body the wounds of the
cross in perpetuity, we pray for those who are deprived
of bodily health, damaged by bodily abuse, worn down
by bodily labors, ashamed of their bodily shape, assaulted
because of the color of their body, or discouraged by
the deterioration of their body, that you would admin-
ister to them the healing powers of your own body and

assure them of the dignity of their individual bodies, so
that by your Spirit they may experience the goodness of
their bodies this day. We pray this in the name of Jesus,
the One whose body redeems and reconciles all human
bodies. Amen.

Before a Surgery

O Lord, you who stretched out your hand in order to
heal the sick and the lame, embrace [Name] with your
tender care this hour, we pray, place your healing hands
upon [him/her], and, through the hands of doctors
and nurses, bless [him/her] with the renewing life of
heaven, so that [he/she] might rest in your shielding
light this day and rise to new life in the aftermath of this
surgery. We pray this in your merciful and compassionate
name. Amen.

For Thanksgiving in the Healing of a Body

O Lord, you who are the Great Physician, we thank you
for healing [Name's] body and for lifting [him/her] out of
the depths, and we ask that you would put a new song in
[Name's] heart, a song of praise to the living God, so that
many might hear of your mighty deed and put their trust in
you. We pray this in the name of Jesus, the One who is the
Resurrection and the Life. Amen.

For Being Instruments of God's Healing in the World

O Lord, you who brought about the healing of the world through your broken body, grace our own broken bodies, we pray, to become instruments of healing to others who have been broken by disease, age, violence, or burnout and who are in need of your healing touch this day, so that we might become your wounded healers wherever we go. We pray this in the name of Jesus, the One who retains the dear tokens of his passion in his body. Amen.

For Those Who Struggle with Mental Health

O Lord, you who are the Father of all mercies and the God of comfort, out of the depths I cry to you this day: find me, I pray, in the chaos of my own brain, preserve me in the storm of my frightened heart, and speak your word of peace to a body that betrays me to disordered and disorientating impulses; be with me and be near me, I beg, so that I may find my home in you even when I am not at home in my own mind. I pray this in the name of the One who walks with me through the darkest valley. Amen.

For Those Who Have Suffered Trauma

O Lord, you who heal the broken of body and soul, we pray for those who have been shattered and scarred by trauma, that you would find them in the depths, hide them in your shelter, comfort them in their pain, protect them from harm, and bind up their wounds, so that they might experience your care this day and be restored in hope to the fullness of life. We pray this in the name of Jesus, the One who extends to us his scarred hands and feet. Amen.

For an Aging Body

O Lord, you who graced the aged to bear new life and the gray-haired to bear witness to your coming, help me, I pray, to endure gracefully the effects of age upon my body and to trust that you still wish to bear new life in and through me, so that I may believe that my gray hairs are a crown of glory and my aged body a gracéd vessel for your salvific work in the world. I pray this in the name of the God of Elizabeth and Zechariah. Amen.

Against a Plague

O Lord, you who are the refuge of the poor and needy, save us, we pray, from the pestilence that stalks in the darkness and the plague that destroys at midday; be our sun and shield; be our fortress; be our comfort this day; may we not fear any evil but rather trust in your might to save and your wisdom to guide, so that we might rest always in the shadow of the Almighty. We pray this in the name of Jesus, the One who heals all our diseases. Amen.

PRAYERS FOR THE VIRTUES AND VICES

The Seven Virtues

For Faith

O Lord, you who are faithful and true, help me, I pray, to trust you with all my heart and not to lean on my own understanding, and where my faith is faint or faulty, help me to believe, dear Lord, so that I may find all my deepest desires satisfied in you alone. I pray this in the name of the One who is trustworthy in all that he promises and faithful in all that he does. Amen.

For Hope

O Lord, you who are the hope of all the ends of the earth, meet me, I pray, in the darkness of my small despairs and speak a word of hope to my anxious heart, so that I might wait faithfully for the fulfillment of your promises in my life and find hope renewed in the hour of my need. I pray this in the name of the One who is the hope of the farthest seas. Amen.

For Love

O Lord, you whose love is unfailing, flood my heart with your love, I pray, and where my heart may be empty or hard, help me to feel afresh my belovedness this day, so that I may be freed to love you and my neighbor with the fearless love of God and thereby fulfill the greatest of all commandments. I pray this in the name of Jesus, the One who has loved me to the end. Amen.

For Prudence

O Lord, you who give wisdom to all who would ask it, may I be wise of heart, teachable of spirit, and care-filled in all my doings, I pray, rather than rash, foolish, or prideful, so that I may discern what is right and good this day for my sake and my neighbor's as well. I pray this in the name of Jesus, the One in whom are hidden all the treasures of wisdom. Amen.

For Fortitude

O Lord, you who strengthen cowardly hearts, make me brave, I pray, in the face of things that terrify and intimidate me, and strengthen my heart in the face of things that try my patience or require my suffering, so that I might become more wholly dependent upon you in the hour of my trial. I pray this in the name of my Redeemer and Defender, Jesus Christ himself. Amen.

For Temperance

O Lord, you who create all things good, increase in me the Spirit's fruit of self-control this day, I pray, so that I may neither indulge nor despise the good gifts of your creation but rather take pleasure in them as you take pleasure in them and share also with others the good gifts of your very Life. I pray this in the name of Jesus, the One who sets us free for love's sake. Amen.

For Justice

O Lord, you who lift up the needy from the ash heap, increase in me a love of justice this day, I pray, so that I, like you, might become one who stands against oppression and inequity, who speaks up for the silenced and who serves as a guardian of the vulnerable. I pray this in the name of Jesus, the Righteous God who brings justice to victory. Amen.

The Seven Vices

For Pride

O Lord, you who oppose the proud but give grace to the humble, help me, I pray, to embrace every occasion this day that deflates my pride, no matter how painful it may be, so that I might more easily walk through the narrow gate that leads to life. I pray this in the name of Jesus, the One who became poor for our sake. Amen.

For Anger

O Lord, you whose love is long-suffering, help me, I pray, to resist this day the temptation to give in to my outbursts of anger and instead to yield my volatile and violent temper to you, so that I may be spared from the destructive ways of the fool and embrace the patient and peaceful ways of the wise. I pray this in the name of the One is rich in love. Amen.

For Envy

O Lord, you who promise to satisfy us with your very self, help me, I pray, to resist the covetous cravings of my heart and grant me the grace to be deeply contented with the good things that are mine, so that I might be delivered from the vain and corrosive powers of jealousy and be freed to delight in all good things, no matter how small they may be. I pray this in the name of the One who satisfies the desires of every living thing. Amen.

For Lust

O Lord, you who satisfy the desires of every living thing, help me, I pray, to resist the possessive lusts of my heart and the disordered appetites of my body, and grant me also the power of your Spirit to honor the holy bodies of others, so that I might experience the proper desires of my own flesh and the true communion of Christ's own love. I pray this in the name of the One at whose right hand are pleasures evermore. Amen.

For Sloth

O Lord, you who are faithful and true, help me, I pray, to resist the fear that you are a Father who would give me only a stone if I asked for bread, leading me to resist your good will for me and to become oppressed by my own apathy; help me instead to believe that you are a good Father who gives good gifts to his children, so that I might be freed from the tyranny of self-indulgent distractions this day. I pray this in the name of the One who wills my good. Amen.

For Greed

O Lord, you who fill us with good things, protect me, I pray, from coveting the glittering images and the glamorous powers of this world, and spare me also from the compulsive need to possess an excess of things, so that I might not fall into the temptation of believing that my happiness rests in the possession of many things. I pray this in the name of the One who fully supplies my every need according to his glorious riches in Jesus Christ. Amen.

For Gluttony

O Lord, you who give us this day our daily bread, protect me, I pray, from gorging myself on food and drink in a way that would turn my belly into a god and my appetite into an idol, and grant me instead the grace to see food and drink as a gift to be shared and savored rather than as an excuse for spiritually rebellious behavior. I pray this in the name of Jesus, the One who gives his flesh as Bread for the life of the world. Amen.

PRAYERS FOR WORK

For a Blessing of the Day's Work

I will not let you go, O Lord, until you bless me;
so bless me this day, this hour, this moment:
Bless my mind to discern the one thing that this
    day requires;
Bless my heart to remain at peace in the face of fear;
Bless my will to resist all needless distractions;
Bless my hands to do the work that you have
    entrusted to me;
Bless my ears to be attuned to your voice;
Bless my eyes to see the signs of your presence;
Bless my feet to go wherever you would lead me.
I pray this so that I might be
like the birds of the air
and the lilies of the field,
free of worry and secure
in the enfolding care
of my Father in heaven.
I pray this in your name.
Amen.

For the Consecration of One's Body for the Labors of the Day

O Lord, you who made us to till and to keep the earth, I offer to you my hands and my feet, my head and my heart, my eyes and my ears and my mouth; consecrate them, I pray, so that I might accomplish the things that you have entrusted to me for this day. I pray this in the name of the One who has made me fearfully and wonderfully. Amen.

For Strength to Accomplish Impossible Tasks

O Lord, you who do the impossible day after day, help me, I pray, to complete the seemingly impossible task that lies before me this day: open my eyes to see what you see and my ears to hear what you hear, strengthen my heart to remain steady in the work that you have committed to me, expand my imagination to perceive what might be and what shall be by grace, and keep my body in health for the work that remains, so that the joy of the Lord might be my strength this day and evermore. I pray this in your Mighty Name. Amen.

For Good Labor when You Do Not Feel Like Laboring but You Need to Get Things Done

O Lord, you who speak a mere word and things come to life, speak, I pray, your creative word into my tired soul and breathe your life-giving power into my sluggish body, so that I might accomplish the good work that you have established for me this day. I pray this in the name of the One who both animates and reanimates my life. Amen.

For Grace to Make the Best of this Day

O Lord, you who know me inside and out, every bone in my body, how I was sculpted from nothing into something, grant me the grace, I pray, to make the best of this day, so that I might work in a non-anxious manner and accomplish your good purposes for me, no more and no less. I pray this in the name of the One who breathes new life into dry bones. Amen.

For Those in Business

O Lord, you who provide food and clothing, gardens and homes, bless, we pray, those who are engaged in the work of making and distributing commercial goods, that they might take joy in their labors, make just use of the earth's resources, and embody the hospitable spirit of your kingdom in the care of their employees, so that the results of their labors may bless the common good in Jesus' name. We pray this in the name of the One who commands us to cultivate and to care for the earth. Amen.

For Minding Our Own Business

O Lord, you who are the True Laborer, help us, we pray, not to make a spectacle of our lives but instead to be content with living a quiet one, minding our own business rather than becoming nosy about others', and working with our hands, so that we might learn gratitude in our own labors. We pray this in the name of Jesus, the One who does all things well. Amen.

For Janitors and Cleaners

O Lord of all pots and pans and things, we give thanks this day for those who clean our houses and our offices, our schools and our parks: grant them, we pray, the gift of your abiding presence, grace them with strength for the labors of the day and the duties of the night, and gift them finally with the praise of heaven and the honor of earth, so that they might know your grace and favor this day. We pray this in the name of Jesus, the Servant of servants. Amen.

For International Workers' Day

O Lord, you who establish the work of our hands, may every labor that we perform this day, whether great or small, thrilling or tedious, public or private, magnificent or modest, be graced by you, we pray, so that our hands might be your loving hands in all that we say and do. We pray this in the name of the True Gardener, Jesus Christ himself. Amen.

For Poll Workers

O Lord, you who come to us as a servant, we pray today for all who serve as poll workers: bless them with

joy, protect them from harm, and shield them from all
wrongful accusations and frustrating technological failures,
so that they may fulfill the good work that you have called
them to do. We pray this in the name of Jesus, the One
who is the servant of all. Amen.

For Monotonous Work

O Lord, you who are infinitely patient, may I not despise
the monotony of this day's work but rather embrace it
as an opportunity to practice the presence of Jesus in the
unseen and unsung labors that are mine to do by grace, so
that I might be faithfully yours in all that I say and do. I
pray this in the name of the One who will reward me according to my labors. Amen.

For Administrative Work

O Lord, you who are the governor of my inbox, the bene-
factor of budgets, the ruler of records, the sovereign of
spreadsheets, and the master of files, grant me the strength,
I pray, to perform my administrative tasks well this day, so
that I might not resent them but rather see them as an occasion to bring order out of chaos. I pray this in the name
of the One who orders all things well. Amen.

For Writing a Sermon

O Lord, you who promise wisdom to all who would ask
it, make me wise, I pray, as I write this sermon today; by

your Spirit make me patient in my labors, surprise me in my study, and guide me in my writing; enlighten also my mind, strengthen my will, enkindle my imagination, and secure in my heart a sincere love for your people, so that I may discern the one thing that you wish speak to them in order that they might encounter your living Word in and through, and perhaps even despite, my own words. I pray this in Jesus' name, humbly releasing the outcome of all my hopes for this sermon to his good purposes. Amen.

For Getting Something Published, Produced, or Picked

O Lord, you who give good gifts to those who would ask it, grant me grace and favor, I pray, in the eyes of those who shall make the final verdict about my work, and guard my heart, I ask, from fear and a crippling disappointment while I wait for an answer, so that I might trust your good purposes for me no matter what may come. I pray this in your Sovereign Name. Amen.

For When Nothing Goes According to Plan

O Lord, you who order all things, grace me, I pray, to make the best of this day that has gone sideways, the serenity to accept the things that I cannot change, and the imagination to see what is possible in the face of all that seems impossible, so that I might persevere with faith in the labors that you have entrusted to me, despite

the fact that nothing about this day has gone according
to plan. I pray this in the name of the Restorer of Broken
Things. Amen.

For Letting Go of All the Woulda, Coulda, Shouldas

O Lord, you who promise that your grace will be sufficient, grant me the grace, I pray, to let go of all the woulda,
coulda, and shouldas that I might accomplish this day and
to do instead the one thing that is most needful, so that I
might do my work under the light of your abundant care. I
pray this in the name of the One who generously clothes
the lilies of the field. Amen.

For the Blessing of Small Labors

O Lord, you who welcomed the humble gift of loaves and
fishes, I offer to you the humble things of this day—my
cleaning, my driving, my tidying, my weeding, my mending,
my ordering, my emailing, my erranding—and ask that you
would bless me in these labors, so that I might be a blessing
to others in all these things. I pray this in the name of the
Good Husbandman. Amen.

For Grocers

O Lord, you who are the True Grocer, bless, we pray, the
farmers who make the food and the manufacturers who
make the goods that we consume; bless the distributors

and the drivers who go the extra mile to make our groceries handy; bless the stockers and the shelvers who put all things in their place; bless the clerks who care for the customers and the cashiers who count their money; bless the baggers and the bakers and the butchers, too; bless the night crews and the day crews; bless also the managers who direct it all; bless these servants, O Lord, each and every one, with your hand of provision and protection. We pray this in the name of Jesus, the One who comes to us as Living Water and Bread of Life. Amen.

For Police Officers

O Lord, you who love righteousness and justice, we pray for all police officers this day, that you would bless them in their duties and strengthen them to defend the cause of the vulnerable, maintain the right of the oppressed, serve the good of the community, and preserve the peace in our cities, so that they might be emissaries of your righteousness and justice in the world. We pray this in the name of the Ruler of the Nations, Jesus Christ himself. Amen.

For a Doctor

O Lord, you who touched the leper and healed the sick, use my hands, I pray, to heal the broken in body and use my words to heal the crushed in spirit, so that I might be an agent of your healing power and restorative care in the

lives of those that you have entrusted to me this day. I pray
this in the name of the Great Physician. Amen.

For Pastors

O Lord, you who are the true Shepherd, we pray for the
shepherds of your church today: be with them in their
hour of need, keep them from evil, restore them, feed them,
and guide them, so that their joy may be renewed in the
work that you have assigned to them by grace. We pray
this in the name of the Bishop of our souls, Jesus Christ
himself. Amen.

For Ministers

O Lord, you who were endowed with the Spirit at your
baptism, attune the ears of your ministers to your Spirit's
voice, we pray, make them wise by your Spirit, and em-
power them to resist a spirit of fear, so that they might
convey the grace of God and speak life-giving words to
your people this day. We pray this in the name of the
Living God. Amen.

For Athletes

O Lord, you who infuse our bodies with vitality, bless
all athletes, we pray, that they might train with hope,
take joy in practice, persevere through pain, and trust
that he who began a good work in them will bring it to
completion. We pray this in the name of the One who

renews our strength so that we might soar on wings like eagles. Amen.

For Those Who Work with Their Hands

O Lord, you who made my hands to till and to keep the earth, bless my hands, I pray, that they may be put to your service and to the service of my neighbor, with loving care and intelligent skill, so that my hands might become the hands of Jesus this day, bringing order out of chaos. I pray this in the name of the One who establishes the work of my hands. Amen.

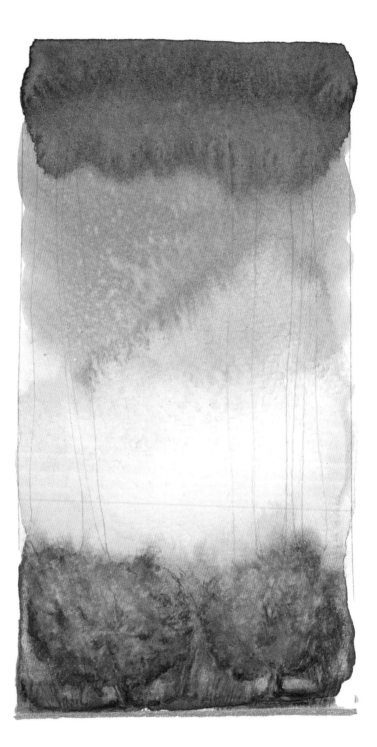

PRAYERS FOR CREATIVES

For the Blessing of the Father

O Father, you who are the Creator of all things, we praise
you for being the source of life, the architect of creation,
and the originator of all good things in heaven and on
earth; grant us fresh ideas, we pray, fill us with new vigor,
and bless our labors, so that we may fulfill your creative
purposes in and through us this day. We pray this in the
name of the Infinitely Imaginative One. Amen.

For the Blessing of the Son

O Christ, you who are Word Made Flesh, we praise you
for sanctifying the earth in your incarnation, confirming
thereby the goodness of the physical world of wood,
stone, metal, wind, and flesh; deliver us this day from
fear, we pray, and save us from the time of trial; teach
us and aid us also in our work today, so that we may be
emissaries of your creative purposes for the earth. We
pray this in the name of Jesus, the One who is the Icon of
God. Amen.

For the Blessing of the Spirit

O Spirit, you who are the Lord and Giver of Life, we praise you for sustaining all things in being, energizing them with vitality and ushering them to their future and final state of glory; purify our souls, we pray, scour our hearts, reorder our minds, and strengthen our bodies, so that we might be freed to be playful in our creative labors this day as befits our status as children of God. We pray this in the name of the One who revives and restores our mortal bodies. Amen.

For Help in the Face of Fears

O Lord, you who strengthen fearful hearts, defend me, I pray, against the fears that bully my heart and grace me to press through my anxieties, so that I might become courageous in the face of the things that terrify and intimidate me and discover new territories of creativity and imagination in my work. I pray this in the Strong Name of Jesus. Amen.

For Help in the Face of Failures

O Lord, you who give strength to the weary, grant me the grace, I pray, to face the failures of my work with humility rather than with pride and to trust that such failures will not result in my shame or ruin but rather in new opportunities for artistry and innovation, so that I might believe that you are the One who miraculously causes something to come out of nothing. I pray this in the name of the One who does infinitely more than we could ask or imagine. Amen.

For Help in the Face of Foes

O Lord, you whose grace is sufficient for all things, make me wise, I pray, to discern the difference between an obstacle and an enemy of my work, and make me brave in the face of my foes, whether little or large, so that I might see such foes as opportunities to become more confident in my work and resilient in my practice. I pray this in the name of the One who enables us to be joyful in hope, patient in affliction, and faithful in prayer. Amen.

For the Blessing of the Holy Trinity

Holy God, Holy Mighty, Holy Immortal, we worship you, we acclaim you, we love you this day; we praise you for the extravagant love that you demonstrate in the creation of this world and ask that you would form us to be a community of artists and creatives that reflects the triune community, so that we might be a people marked by self-giving love, infectious joy, and the desire to honor and glorify your name for the sake of this world that you so love. We pray this in the name of the Father, the Son, and the Holy Spirit. Amen.

PRAYERS FOR SCHOOL

For Children Going to School

Dear Jesus, you who promise to be with me always, I pray
that you would be with me this day as I go to school;
bless my going and my coming, bless my learning and my
playing; protect my heart from fear, keep me safe, and give
me good friends, so that I might experience the fullness of
your joy this day and evermore. I pray this in the name of
Jesus, the One who loves me from head to toe. Amen.

For Homeschooled Kids

Dear Jesus, you who promise to be with me always, I pray
that you would be with me at home this day as I do my
schoolwork; bless my learning and my playing, help me to do
my best, help me not to feel alone, and help me, I pray, to be
patient with my family, so that I might experience the fullness
of your joy this day and evermore. I pray this in the name of
Jesus, the One who loves me from head to toe. Amen.

For High School and College Students

O Lord, you who promise to be with me always, be with
me this day as I begin my schoolwork; keep me in health,

I pray, and keep me from harm; and in all that I say and do, may I love you with all of my heart, soul, mind, and strength, and may I love my neighbor as myself, so that I might fulfill your calling upon my life as a student. I pray this in Christ's name. Amen.

For Teachers

O Lord, you who have called and equipped the teachers in our community, bless them this day, we pray; watch over them, guide and sustain them, and instill in them a sincere love for their students, so that they together may be astonished by the wonder of this world and be stirred afresh to live wisely in it. We pray this in the name of Christ our Teacher. Amen.

For Oneself as a Teacher

O Lord, you who are the Good Teacher, I thank you for calling me to this important work of teaching others; help me, I pray, to love my students and to be patient with the things that do not go according to plan, and may I help my students to become humble in the face of ignorance, to delight in things newly discovered, and to love the truth with all of their hearts and minds, so that they might be wise and compassionate citizens in this world that you so love. I pray this in the name of Jesus, the One who is the Truth. Amen.

For School Administrators

O Lord, you who have promised wisdom to all who would ask it, we pray today for school administrators, that you would grant them clarity of mind, strength of will, resilience of body, a heart of wisdom, and the gift of your truth-bearing Spirit, so that they might be enabled to make decisions that lead to the flourishing of their teachers, staff, and students and to the well-being of the whole community. We pray this in the name of Jesus, the Rabbi of Nazareth. Amen.

For Parents Sending Their Children Off to a New School

O Lord, you who promise to guide us through the wilderness and to protect us through the storm, make us brave, we pray, where we feel afraid, make us strong in the face of our weaknesses, and make possible what to us seems impossible, so that we might joyfully entrust ourselves and our children into your tender care as they go off to school and fulfill your good purposes for them in this new season of life. We pray this in the good name of Jesus. Amen.

Before Taking a Test

O Lord, you who are merciful and kind, bless me, I pray, as I take this test, that I might recall all that I have studied, do my best, be free of worry, and never forget that my life is in your hands, so that I might experience the peace that surpasses all understanding. I pray this in the name of the One who will complete the good purposes that he began in me long ago. Amen.

Before Grading a Test or a Paper

O Lord, you who judge all things fairly, grant me a clear mind and a humble heart as I do my work of grading this day, I pray, so that I might hold the lives of my students with the same care that you hold my own. I pray in the name of the Just and Merciful One, Jesus Christ himself. Amen.

For Graduates

O Lord, you who guide and govern all our days, we pray for our graduates this day: may all that they have learned in this season of study increase in them a love of wisdom, may the skills that they have acquired result in a love of the work that you have entrusted to them, and may the relationships that have marked this period of life increase in them a love of neighbor; bless them in the days to come, we pray, be near to them in their hour of need, surround them with kindred friends, grant them the desires of their hearts, and fulfill your good purposes for them in their life and work, so that they might become a blessing to this world that you so love. We pray this in the name of the One who brings all things to a good end, Jesus Christ himself. Amen.

PRAYERS FOR MUNDANE LIFE

For Beginnings

O Lord, you who are the Author of all good beginnings, bless, I pray, the beginning of this new venture and grant me the ability to trust that you go before me in all things, so that I might give myself fully to the work ahead and hope for a good outcome in the end. I pray this in the name of Jesus, the One who is the Beginning and the End. Amen.

For God's Daily Care

O Lord, you who know your sheep by name, be my Shepherd this day, I pray; where I am burdened by the cares of life, grant me rest, where I am harassed and helpless against the enemies of my soul, be my defender, and where I am weary, restore me; guard me, keep me, shield me, O Christ, so that I might feel your loving care this day. I pray this in the name of Jesus, the One who lays down his life for his sheep night and day. Amen.

Before a Meal

O Lord, you who sustain us from the bounty of the earth, we thank you for this meal: may it nourish and strengthen us, and may we always remain thankful to those who farm, make, and distribute this food and this drink, so that we may be generous in all that we say and do. We pray this in Jesus' name. Amen.

For Discerning the Will of God

O Lord, you who guide me in the way everlasting, grant me the ability to hear your voice, I pray, the wisdom to know the way forward, the courage to choose it, and the humility to accept it as your good, pleasing, and perfect will for me. I pray this in the name of the One who establishes my steps in love and sets me within the company of the wise. Amen.

For Those Who Feel Vulnerable

O Lord, you who are the God of Angel Armies, hear my prayer; where I am defenseless, be my defender; where I am exposed, be my refuge; where I am vulnerable, be my shield; and where I am scared, be my comfort, so that I might feel safe this day within the sanctuary of your sheltering wings. I pray this in the name of Jesus, the Lion of the Tribe of Judah. Amen.

For the Blessing of Little Deeds of Faith

O Lord, you who do not despise the day of small things, we offer to you this day our little but faltering efforts at daily prayer, our simple acts of obedience in the face of temptations to do otherwise, and our small deeds of love that may go unnoticed or unthanked, and ask that you would bless them, so that we might know the joy of loving you in and through all such little things. We pray this in the name of Jesus, the One who became small for our sakes. Amen.

For Knowing When to Say No to One More Thing That You Want to Do, Because It Will Probably Be Bad for Your Mental, Physical, and Relational Health

O Lord, you who promise wisdom to those who would ask it, help me, I pray, to discern the difference between what I *can* be doing and *should* be doing, and grant me the fortitude to say no in the face of pressures that would tell me to do otherwise, so that I might discover the gift of limits and the grace of less being truly more. I pray this in the name of Jesus, the One who travels to some but not to all the villages of Israel. Amen.

For a Sporting Game (After Nick Comiskey)

O God of Conquest, you who train our hands for war and our fingers for battle, guide and direct us, we pray, that we might play our very best, conduct ourselves with dignity, and by your grace drink deeply of the sweet marrow of victory. We pray this through the only Name under heaven by which we are saved, win or lose, now and forever, Jesus Christ himself. Amen.

For When Things Don't Go According to Plan

O Lord, you who grant us the desires of our heart and make our plans to succeed, take my bitter disappointment, I pray, in the plans that did not succeed and the desires that have not been fulfilled, and breathe a fresh word of hope into my soul, so that I might not lose heart and give up altogether. I pray this in the name of the One who directs my steps. Amen.

For the One Who Feels Disoriented in Life

O Lord, you who have numbered the hairs on my head, speak a word of hope to my heart, I pray, so that I might feel seen and heard by you in this place of disorientation and displacement and where a sense of purposelessness seems to mark every aspect of my life. I pray this in the name of the One who has ordained all the days of my life. Amen.

For Bleary-Eyed Parents

O Lord, you who hold all things together, help me, I pray, not to lose my mind; you who calmed the tempest, help me not to lose my temper; you who promised rest to the

weary, speak a word of peace to my tired body; you who
healed the blind, open my eyes to see your presence in
the dark; you who speak things into life, help me to hear
your small voice over the din of my own noisy mind; you
who welcomed the children, take care of my own; and you
who promised to be with us always, be with me here and
now in my hour of need, so that I may feel your tangible
care. I pray this in the name of Jesus, the Compassionate
One. Amen.

After a Restless Night of Sleep

O Lord, you who are my sun and shield, speak your
word of peace, I pray, to the thoughts of my mind after a
troubled night of sleep, which has left my heart disturbed
and my body agitated, so that I might abide in your sustaining care this day. I pray this in the name of the Captain
of my Salvation, Jesus Christ himself. Amen.

In the Aftermath of a Bad Dream

O Lord, you who deliver us from evil, wipe from my heart
the residue of last night's nightmare and purge my mind of
its oppressive memory, I pray, so that I might be delivered
from its menacing presence and be freed to live this day
under the light of your radiant truth. I pray this in the
name of Jesus, the One who stands sovereign over all the
forces of chaos. Amen.

For Not Doing Great Things for God
(After Douglas McKelvey)

O Lord, you who see all things, help me to be okay, I pray, with the fact that I have done nothing great for you this day, or for anybody else, so that I might be at peace with the littleness of my life and trust that you love me no matter what. I pray this in the name of the One who feeds the birds of the air. Amen.

Against Living in an Economy of Scarcity

O Lord, you who own the cattle on a thousand hills, preserve us from living in an economy of scarcity, we pray, where nothing and no one is good enough, causing us to live stingy and self-absorbed lives; fill our hearts instead with your abundant life, so that we may be generous-spirited in all that we do and say this day. We pray this in the name of the True Vintner. Amen.

For Being Need-full of God

O Lord, you who care for the birds of the air, cause us to laugh today, we pray, because we have discovered that we no longer need to be lonely in the anxiety of our own self-reliance, so that we might delight in the freedom of utter dependence upon you and in our need of your complete care. We pray this in the name of the Clothier of Lilies. Amen.

For Things that Seem Impossible

O Lord, you who are able to accomplish far more than we could ever ask or imagine, help us, we pray, to ask for the right things and to imagine what may seem impossible to us but that, to you, is fully possible, so that we may witness your power at work in and through us this day. We pray this in the name of the One who makes a way through the Red Sea. Amen.

For Being Wise to Say No

O Lord, you who tell us to pray for daily bread, help me to be wise and brave, I pray, to say no to the things that are not needful for this day and to say yes to the things that can and should be done, so that I may remain faithful to your good, pleasing, and perfect will for me this day. I pray this in the name of the One who stores up wisdom for the upright. Amen.

For Making Broth

O Lord, you who spat upon the dirt in order to make mud that would heal a blind man's eyes, bless, I pray, these elements of earth—water and fire, root and leaf, fish and fowl, spirit and spice—so that by the powers that you have vested in nature and enlivened by your Spirit, they might heal and restore all who drink it. I pray this in the name of the One who sends ravens to Elijah to deliver him bread and meat both night and day. Amen.

For a Day That's Going Only Wrong

O Lord, you who bring order out of chaos, take all the things that are going wrong with this day, I pray, and speak your word of peace to my anxious heart and your word of order to my confused mind, so that I might assuredly know that your right hand upholds me, even as I cling to you for dear life. I pray this in the name of Jesus, the One who stills the storm with a word. Amen.

For the Proper Numbering of Our Days

O Lord, you who teach us to number our days so that we may gain a heart of wisdom, help me, I pray, not to become obsessed with numbering every minute of the day in order to become maximally productive but rather to trust that your grace is sufficient for the day's task, so that I might work in peace and live in grace. I pray this in the name of Jesus, the Faithful Witness. Amen.

For the Little Things

O Lord, you who welcomed the little gifts of bread and fish, we offer to you this day our own little gifts—our little accomplishments, our little acts of service, our little words of love, our little moments of faithfulness, our little efforts to grow and to learn—and ask that you would bless them, so that they might serve your good purposes beyond anything that we could ask or imagine. We pray this in the name of the One who delights in all the little things. Amen.

For Little Deeds of Kindness to Another

O Lord, you who do not despise the day of small things, prompt us by your Spirit, we pray, to speak a little word of kindness to our family this day and to offer a little act of care to a friend, so that we might not think that your love is made manifest only in big things. We pray this in the name of Jesus, the One who is born in the little town of Bethlehem. Amen.

For a Grumpy Mood

O Lord, you who rescue us from the pit, rescue me, I pray, from this grumpy mood, with all its black clouds and ir-ritable feelings, causing me to see only what is wrong with this day and to find everything and everybody wanting, so that I might see this day right-side up and marked by your goodness. I pray this in the name of the One who restores all things broken. Amen.

For Changing a Diaper at Night

O Lord, you who keep watch with me through the hours of this night, bless my hands, I pray, as I change [Name's] diaper, precious to me and beloved to you, so that I might offer to [Name] the same care that you have offered to me. I pray this in the name of the One who watches over all who love him. Amen.

For Getting Shots at the Doctor

O Lord, you who comfort children with your healing presence, protect and comfort my children, I pray, as they receive their shots right now, so that they might not be terrified by the experience but rather know, here and now, your loving power to heal and to restore. I pray this in the name of the One who makes both bodies and antibodies. Amen.

For the Blessing of All My Senses

O Lord, you who make all things good, may my eyes see others kindly this day, my ears hear the heart behind the words that are said, my nose delight in the scents of your creation, my tongue savor the goodness of everything that I eat and drink, and my hands bring a healing touch to all whom I meet, so that I may be your very body in all that I do and say. I pray this in the name of the One who sanctifies me body and soul. Amen.

For Going on Vacation (After Ray Simpson)

O Lord, you who promise to be with us in our coming and our going, we ask your blessing upon us as we begin this vacation; help us to release to you all that we leave behind: the people that we love, the pressures that weary us, the tasks that we left unfinished, and the problems that would hound and haunt us; help us also to embrace all that you would have for us: the joy of adventure, the delight of

companionship, the laughter of play, the rest of soul, and
the discovery of beauty; and may we be refreshed in our
going and replenished in our coming. We pray this in the
name of the One who delights to give his children good
gifts. Amen.

For Thanksgiving on Behalf of Those Who Are Faithful in the Little Things

O Lord, you who see what we do in secret, we celebrate
this day those who remain faithful in little things: we ap-
plaud their unseen deeds of love, we cherish their hidden
gestures of kindness, we laud their resolve to hope in
the face of despair, and we praise you for their witness
to joy; we ask also that you would bless them, so that
they might be assured of your everlasting affections for
them this day. We pray this in the name of the God Who
Sees. Amen.

For Being Present to the Present

O Lord, you who tell us not to worry about tomorrow, help
us, we pray, to be present to the present this day, neither
fretting about what is past nor worrying about what is to
come, but rather trusting in your wisdom to guide and your
grace to sustain, so that we might live and work in peace
this day. We pray this in the name of the One who knows
all our needs. Amen.

For Mere Mortals Like Ourselves

O Lord, you who have set your glory in the heavens, may
we look to the sky above, the earth below, and the seas
beyond in order to see how very small we are as mortals,
we pray, so that we might also feel how very special we are
in your eyes. We pray this in the name of the One who
crowns us with glory and honor. Amen.

For Daily Bread

O Lord, you who are the Bread of Life, help us, we
pray, to be content with the bread that you give us
this day, neither grasping for more, for fear of being in
want tomorrow, nor shrinking away, for fear that we
do not deserve it, so that we might feel sated with your
good provision. We pray this in the name of God our
Provider. Amen.

For a Job Interview

O Lord, you who bestow grace and favor upon those who
walk with integrity, grant me the grace, I pray, to do my
level best in this interview, and give me favor in the eyes
of all whom I shall meet, so that I may feel at peace with
the outcome, trusting fully in your good purposes for me. I
pray this in the name of Immanuel, the God who is with
me. Amen.

For Exhausted Mothers and Fathers

O Lord, you who looked tenderly upon the daughters of
Jerusalem in their hour of need, look tenderly upon me
in my own, I pray: upon a brain that repeatedly forgets
the details, a heart that is burdened by countless worries,
a body that betrays me to perpetual weariness, a temper
that runs shorter and shorter, a will that grows faint with
purpose, and a soul that has grown indifferent to spiritual
matters; grant me, I pray, your tender touch upon my
weary bones, your gift of peace to a troubled mind, and
your resurrecting hope in the deepest places of my being,
so that I might experience your tangible care in this
dark and lonely valley. I pray this in the name of Jesus,
the One who lays down his life for his sheep night and
day. Amen.

For a Conference

O Lord, you in whom all things hold together, bless our
conference, we pray, and hold in grace all that we do and
say, so that our gathering might be held together in love
and result in good gifts beyond our imagining, for the
strengthening of our common bonds and for the blessing
of this world that you so love. We pray this in the name of
the One who is able to accomplish abundantly more than
we could ever ask or imagine. Amen.

For Journeying to a New Home

O Lord, you who called Abraham to travel to a strange place that would become his true home, go before us on this journey to a new home, we pray, and grant us the grace to trust you to establish us in a foreign place, so that, in time, this new place might become a familiar place for our true flourishing. We pray this in the name of Jesus, the One who is our True Home forever. Amen.

Against "Settling" in Life

O Lord, you who promise to refresh and to sustain those who weary of doing good, protect me this day, I pray, from the temptation to settle for lesser or false loves, and rescue me from a heart of despair on account of the sorrows and losses of life, so that I might find my rest in you and the courage to do what is right and good. I pray this in your gracious name. Amen.

For Silence

O Lord, you who stand sovereign over the chaos of this world, speak, I pray, a word of peace to the noise that confuses my mind, soothe the agitation of my body and make my heart a holy habitation for the still, small voice of your Spirit, so that I may experience the peace of God that guards my heart and mind. I pray this in the name of the One meets us in the silence. Amen.

For Endings

O Lord, you who bring all our endings to a good end, may you be our True End at the end of this day, we pray, and may the ending of our life's journey find us more fully at home with you, so that we may experience you as our Deepest Desire this day and forever more. We pray this in the name of Jesus, the One who makes his dwelling with us. Amen.

PRAYERS FOR PUBLIC LIFE

For Being Heralds of Good News

O Lord, you who are the Author of all goodness, make us, we pray, heralds of your good news, signposts of your good name, instruments of your good work, and a foretaste of the fullness of goodness in the age to come for those who do not know you today, so that all who encounter us might know and love you. We pray this in the name of Jesus our Redeemer. Amen.

For Reading the Not-So-Good News

O Lord, you who are the herald of good news, help me, I pray, to read the news of this day not cynically but with faith, not despairingly but with hope, and not indifferently but with love, so that I might glimpse and bear witness to your good work in the world. I pray this in the name of the Sovereign of History. Amen.

To Be Said After Reading Bad News

O Lord, you who hold all things together in your sovereign care, help me, I pray, to perceive how you are at work in this broken world, the empirical evidence notwithstanding, show me again how to love my neighbor as myself, and shore up hope in my heart, so that I might live trustingly this day. I pray this in the name of Jesus, the One Who Is Always Near at Hand. Amen.

For Driving in Traffic

O Lord, you who come and go as you please, I do not come and go as I please, but go to work when I must and come home when I can; be with me, I pray, in the unpredictable and oft-wearying transit back and forth, so that I might know your peace that surpasses all the stresses of this traffic. I pray this in the name of the One who goes before me and behind me. Amen.

For Being Virtuous on Social Media

O Lord, you who warn us that the tongue is a fire, make me quick to listen, I pray, slow to post, and even slower to post in anger, so that my tongue might not become a restless evil, full of deadly poison. I pray this in the name of the God to whom I shall have to give an account on the day of judgment for every careless word that I have uttered on social media. Amen.

For Being Like the Care-Filled Jesus

O Lord, you who washed feet, made breakfast, mended bodies, touched the untouchables, ate with the undesirables, nurtured the little ones, cast out demons, healed the sick, taught the crowds, freed the captives, wept openly, shared liberally, and loved freely: help me, I pray, to be like you so that I might care for others this day as you in your mercy have cared for me. I pray this in the name of Jesus, the One who leaves us an example that we should follow. Amen.

For Not Being Ashamed of Jesus in Public

O Lord, you whose kindness exceeds our capacity to grasp, have mercy, we pray, upon our cowardly ways and our tendencies to deny you in public, so that we might not run away from you in the face of fear but draw near to the One who loves us to the end. We pray this in the name of Jesus, the One who is the Light and Life of the nations. Amen.

For Those Experiencing Food Insecurity

O Lord, you who miraculously provided for the widow at Zarephath, we pray for those who are experiencing food insecurity this day and ask that, as with the feeding of the five thousand, you would not only make provision for them but also use us to be your hands and feet, generously providing for those in need, so that we together might experience your extraordinary hospitality. We pray this in the name of Jesus, the Advocate of our Faith. Amen.

For the Installation of a New Head of State

O Lord, you who raise up and remove kings, we pray for the peaceful transition of power this day and ask that you would make wise the rulers of this country, that they might execute both justice and peace on behalf of its people, so that we might be a nation that bears witness to the shalom of God. We pray this in the name of Jesus, the One who is enthroned in heaven. Amen.

For the Political Tempests of Our World

O Lord, you who are the lover of concord, help us, we pray, not to become needlessly anxious over the political tempests that rage across the landscape of our land but rather to trust in your providential care, so that we might remain peacemakers to friend and stranger alike this day. We pray this in the name of Jesus, the One who holds all things together. Amen.

For Our Wounded Country

O Lord, you who are the Wounded Healer, we offer to you our wounded lives, our wounded neighborhoods, and our wounded country this day and we ask that you would mend them, so that we might know you as the One who consoles the brokenhearted and heals our broken communities. We pray this in the name of the One who binds up the bruises of his people. Amen.

For Grace Between Fellow Believers Across Political Lines

O Lord, you who prayed that we might be one as you and the Father are one, grant us the grace this day, we pray, to extend the right hand of fellowship to fellow saints across political lines, so that a watching world may see that your Spirit's power is far greater than all the fracturing powers that would keep us separated and suspicious of one another. We pray this in the name of Jesus, the One who reconciles all things. Amen.

For 9/11

O Lord, you who are the God of the living and the dead, we thank you for all who sacrificed their lives in the service of others on 9/11, we pray that you would heal all lingering traumatic memories, and we ask that you would mend all relations that remain broken still between neighbor and nation, so that we might work toward a day on which nation shall not lift up sword against nation. We pray this in the name of Jesus, the Prince of Peace. Amen.

For the Victims of War

O Lord, you who raise the needy from the ash heap, have mercy, we pray, upon the widow, the orphan, the poor, and the oppressed, so that they might not fear the arrow that flies by day nor the terror of night, but rather know your powerful and protective care this day. We pray this in the name of the One who lifts all those who are bowed down. Amen.

For the War-Weary

O Lord, you who see and set the world's chaos right, be a safe house, we pray, for the battered and beaten this day and a sanctuary for the exhausted and exposed, so that they might sense your care by day and sing your song of deliverance by night. We pray this in the name of the One who shields and shepherds the poor and needy by his right hand. Amen.

For the Welfare of Our Cities

O Lord, you who charge us to seek the welfare of the city, strengthen us, we pray, to work for the good of our neighbor, the health of institutions that sustain our society, and the vitality of organizations that contribute to the well-being of all people, so that the engines of culture in our country might become a reflection of your life-giving kingdom and lead to the flourishing of all peoples. We pray this in the name of Jesus, the One who does all things well. Amen.

Against the Uproar of the Nations

O Lord, you who raise up kings and remove kings, keep despair at bay, we pray, preserve our tongues from evil, let our hope remain in you, and may we not forget that you are sovereign over the temerity of human pride, so that we might be at peace in the face of the uproar of our world. We pray this in the name of the One who laughs at the vanity of nations. Amen.

For the Blessing of the Nations

O Lord, you from whom every family in heaven and on earth derives its name, bless the nations this day, we pray, and use us to bear witness to your glory in all the peoples of earth, so that your ways may be known upon the earth and the nations might be glad and sing for joy. We pray this in the name of the One around whom representatives of every tongue, tribe, and nation shall gather in praise forever more, Jesus Christ himself. Amen.

PRAYERS FOR
RELATIONAL LIFE

For Speaking a Word of Blessing
to All Whom I Meet

O Lord, you who from whom all blessings flow, may my
mouth be full of blessing this day, I pray, speaking a blessing
to my family at home, to my friends near and far, to the
stranger on the way and to the enemy in the way, so that I
might become a living beatitude for Christ's sake. I pray this
in the name of the One who commands our blessing. Amen.

For Unity (After Psalm 133)

O Lord, you who promise your blessing of unceasing life
when we choose to live together in unity, grant us the grace
this day to love one another sacrificially, we pray, and to
think the best rather than the worst of each other, so that
we might be an icon of the Trinity to a watching world. We
pray this in the name of the Indivisible God. Amen.

For the Gift of Good Community

O Lord, you who make a home for the homeless, grant us
the gift of good community, we pray, so that we might find

our place there, secure in the knowledge that we are deeply loved and in turn generously welcome others to share in that same love for the sake of the One who calls us brothers and sisters. We pray this in the name of the Holy Trinity. Amen.

For the Beloved Community

O Lord, you whose love is without measure, help us, we pray, to love as you love, by befriending the friendless, defending the defenseless, caring for the careless, and showing mercy to the merciless, so that we might become your beloved community in word and in deed this day. We pray this in the name of our Messiah King, Jesus Christ himself. Amen.

For Seeing Each Other as a Provision of Grace

O Lord, you who called to yourself apostles who never imagined that they would have anything in common with each other, open our eyes, we pray, to see our nearby brothers and sisters as your provision of grace rather than as always wanting, so that we might become surprising gifts of grace to one another this day. We pray this in your gracious name. Amen.

For Single Parents

O Lord, you who are the God Who Sees, have compassion, we pray, upon the single parents in our community, provide for them out of the storehouse of your bounty, and be near to them in their loneliness; cause us also, we pray, to become your provision of familial grace to them, so that we might be knit together as your family in mutual care. We pray this in the name of the God of Hagar and Naomi. Amen.

For Strained Relationships

O Lord, you who love us to the very end, grant us your Spirit of power today, we pray, so that we might speak a word of blessing to those who think poorly of us, serve those who wish us the worst and bear gently with family and friends who may judge us in haste. We pray this in the name of Jesus, the One who in his flesh breaks down all walls of hostility. Amen.

For Grace in the Face of Contentious Relationships

O Lord, you who command us to turn the other cheek, we pray that our disagreements with family, arguments with friends, and troubling encounters with strangers will bring out the best rather than the worst in us, so that we might be living emblems of your gracious kingdom in a chronically graceless time. We pray this in the name of Jesus, the Prince of Life. Amen.

For a Strained Christmas Day Family Meal

O Lord, you who call us brothers and sisters, have mercy, I pray, upon my family, keep us from strife, guard us from suspicion, and protect us from indifference; grace me also to bear all things and to hope all things in love, so that we might not become foreigners to one another on this Christmas Day. We pray this in the name of Jesus, the Peace-Bearing Child. Amen.

For a Strained Family Thanksgiving

O Lord, you who are the God of impossible things, grant me the grace, I pray, to love the unlovable parts of my family in our time together this Thanksgiving Day, even as I confess in humility to the unlovable parts in myself, so that I might be at peace with them as far as it is possible. I pray this in the name of Jesus, the Chief Shepherd of our souls. Amen.

For Those Who Do Not Feel at Home in Their Own Family

O Lord, you who have known the heartache of misunderstanding from family members, I offer up to you my fragile and disconsolate heart and ask that you would be with me this day, I pray, so that I might know deep in my bones that I belong forever to the family of God. I pray this in the name of Jesus, the One who never abandoned his own. Amen.

For Enduring Hard Things with Extended Family Members

O Lord, you who were frustrated by your own family, have mercy, I pray, upon my family and grant me the grace to

do what seems impossible—to bear all things, to believe
all things, to hope all things, and to endure all things—so
that we together might experience your ministry of reconciliation this day. I pray this in the name of Jesus, the One
who makes all things new. Amen.

For Reconciliation with a Fellow Believer

O Lord, you who are able to do far more than I could ask
or imagine, help me, I pray, to be kind and compassionate
to my fellow believer when I would rather hold on to
resentment and judgment, so that we together may experience the beauty and power of your reconciling love. We
pray this in the name of Jesus, the One who is the Head of
the Church. Amen.

For the Blessing of a Marriage

O Lord, you who cause the two to become one flesh, we
thank you for this marriage and we ask that you might
bless it, so that their life together might become a reflection
of Divine Love that always protects, always trusts, always
hopes, and always perseveres. We pray this in the name of
Jesus, the One whose love never fails. Amen.

For a Bad Patch in a Marriage

O Lord, you whose love surpasses all that we could ever
imagine, heal and restore my marriage, I pray, and enable
me to imagine what it could be by grace, so that I might

remain faithful to the one whom I love and to the one whom you love even more so. I pray this in the name of the One who does the impossible day after day and night after night. Amen.

For a Struggling Marriage

O Lord, you whose love is as strong as death, grant me the grace, I pray, to trust as you trust, to hope as you hope, and to love as you love, so that my marriage might be rescued from harm and be renewed this day by your grace, for our sake and for the sake of the ones whom we love. I pray this in the name of Jesus, the One who loves us to the very end. Amen.

For the Newly Divorced

O Lord, you who make a home for the widow and the orphan, have mercy upon me in my loneliness: heal my hurting heart, I pray, and deliver me from despair, so that I may yet hope that goodness and lovingkindness shall follow me all the days of my life. I pray this in the name of Jesus, the One who sees and cares. Amen.

For the Forgiveness of Sin
Against One's Neighbor

O Lord, you whose mercies are new every morning, forgive me, I pray, for any unkind word, any impatient gesture, any selfish deed, any failure to show sympathy, and any omission of kindness that I have committed this day, so that I may be filled anew with your Spirit's power to love as Jesus loves. I pray this in the name of Jesus, the merciful Mediator of all. Amen.

For Strength to Forgive Those Who Have Hurt Us

O Lord, you who charge us to forgive others not seven but seventy-seven times, help us, we pray, to do the impossible by your Spirit's power: to forgive those who have wounded us, so that we might become recipients of your grace and agents of your peaceable kingdom this day. We pray this in the name of Jesus, the Prince of Peace. Amen.

For Struggling to Ask for Forgiveness

O Lord, you who promise to aid us in our weakness, make us brave and humble of heart, we pray, so that we might ask and receive forgiveness from the one we have harmed and so become, like Jesus, a peacemaker. We pray this in the name of the One who both charges and empowers us to forgive as God in Christ has forgiven us. Amen.

For the Blessing of One's Friends

O Lord, you who have blessed us with the gift of friendship, we pray today for our friends, that they would experience your grace in specific and special ways, so that they might tangibly know that you are with them and for them in all that they do. We pray this in the name of Jesus, the One who calls us friends. Amen.

For Being a True Friend

O Lord, you who did not give up on your fickle and faithless friends, help me, I pray, not to give up on my friends but rather by your grace to bear with them, to believe in them, to hope for them, and to endure alongside them, so that I might be a true friend for love's sake. I pray this in the name of Jesus, the One who everlastingly befriends me. Amen.

Before a Hard Conversation with a Friend

O Lord, you who promise to be with me always, be with me in this conversation, I pray, that your Spirit might make me brave, wise, and humble, that I might speak in love and listen in love, and that we both might hear and heed the truth that would set us equally free, so that we might experience your life-giving power this day. We pray this in your mighty name. Amen.

For the Friendless

O Lord, you who named your disciples friends rather than servants, be with all this day who feel afraid and alone, we pray; grace us also to be your body in word and in deed to the lonely in our community, so that we might bring your word of hope to the friendless and the forsaken. We pray this in the name of Jesus, the One who promises not to leave us as orphans but to provide us with the care and comfort of his Spirit. Amen.

For the Lonely Single Person

O Lord, you who were alone in the wilderness, be with me, I pray, in this time of singleness, and when I feel tempted to believe that I have been abandoned by friends or forsaken by God, may I sense the sweet presence of your Spirit nourishing me in my hour of need, so that I might know that I am never alone but filled and fortified by your very presence. I pray this in the name of the One who deals tenderly with the lonely sparrows of this world. Amen.

For a Hard Conversation Between Pastor and Parishioner

O Lord, you who rebuked Peter in love and who gently chided James and John, grant me the grace, I pray, to do this hard conversation well and to trust that you will be the Shepherd that we all desperately need, so that we together may experience your severe mercy as a form of benevolent love. We pray this in your gracious and compassionate name. Amen.

Before a Hard Meeting

O Lord, you who warned us that we would have trouble in this world, we confess to you our worries over things that we cannot control, our distress over things that seem wrong-headed, and our frustration with those who oppose us on things that we hold dearly; grant us, we pray, the ability to bear with one another in love, and may the peace of God guard our hearts and minds, so that together we might trust your leading and walk in the way of unity that only the Spirit of Christ can make possible. We pray this in your gracious name. Amen.

For Being Delivered from What-about-ism

O Lord, you who told Peter to mind his own business and not to worry about what happened to John, deliver us, we pray, from the infection of what-about-ism and help us to trust instead that you will do right by each of us in the end, so that we may fix our eyes this day on the pioneer and perfecter of our faith. We pray this in the name of our Just Judge. Amen.

To Be Merciful Rather than Vindictive

O Lord, you whose mercies are new every morning, grant me your Spirit's help this day, I pray, to be merciful rather than vindictive with those who have failed or wronged me in any way, so that I may be counted among your blessed people. I pray this in the name of the One to whom alone belongs vengeance. Amen.

For the Blessing of a Retreat

O Lord, you who retreated to a quiet place in order to rest and to recover with your disciples, bless our retreat, we pray; grant us also the gift of joyful play, sanctify our festive meals, deepen our kindred relations, be present to our leisurely conversation, and nurture our souls with spiritual foods, so that we might return to our places of work and home revitalized by your Spirit of Life. We pray this in the name of the God who restores and renews us. Amen.

PRAYERS FOR A VIOLENT WORLD

After a Mass Shooting

O Lord, you who abhor the bloodthirsty and violent, be not deaf to our bitter cries, we pray, and do not abandon us to our pain this day; hear our raging words of protest, heed our groans for justice, and meet us in this lowly and desperate place. *Awake, Lord! Rouse yourself! Deliver us from evil for your name's sake!* We pray this so that we might witness your might to save and your power to heal. We pray this in the name of our Fortress and our Refuge. Amen.

For Enemies

O Lord, you who ask us to do the impossible—to bless our enemies, to pray for those who persecute us, and to love those who seek us harm—we pray that you would do the impossible in us, to enable us to love our enemies as you love them and to remember who our true enemy is: sin, death, and the devil. Perform also a miracle in the hearts of our enemies, so that we together might experience the power of your reconciling Spirit this day. We pray this in the name of Jesus, the One who overcomes evil with good. Amen.

Against Bloodthirstiness

O Lord, you who detest the bloodthirsty, subdue the murderous, we pray, break the sword of the violent, and rebuke a culture of death that would make bloodthirstiness flourish in our land, so that we might witness you this day as the God of Justice and the Lord of Righteousness under the light of the noonday sun. We pray this in the name of Christ our King and Prince of Peace. Amen.

Against Our Own Violent Impulses

O Lord, you who promise a day in which there will be no more violence in the land, stay the hand of violence in our own lives, we pray; keep violent words from our lips, detain our hands and feet from violent actions, and deliver us from the impulse to indulge violent thoughts in the privacy of our own consciences, so that we might be worthy to be called children of God this day, blessed in our peacemaking ways. We pray this in the name of Jesus, the Prince of Peace. Amen.

To Become a Justice-Loving People

O Lord, you who hate those who record unjust decisions, may we be a people who stand against injustice that occurs anywhere as a threat to justice everywhere, so that we might become worthy representatives of your righteous kingdom and extremists for Christ's love this day. We pray this in the name of Jesus, the One who sets the oppressed free. Amen.

For Those Who Weary of Doing Justice

O Lord, you who see the hearts of all with perfect clarity, I confess this day my irritation with those who bully their way with words, who think that none see what they do in the shadows, and who traffic in violence; strengthen my weary body, I pray, minister to my angry spirit and comfort my fearful heart, so that I might not lose hope in doing the right thing in the name of justice. I pray this in the name of the God who is Holy and Just. Amen.

For Peace in a Time of War

O Lord, you who are the True King, have mercy, we pray, upon the war-torn peoples of the world; silence also the warmongers, scatter the bloodthirsty, shatter the weapons of war, and take pity upon the vulnerable, so that true peace and justice might be restored to this land. We pray this in the name of Jesus, the Prince of Peace. Amen.

Of Allegiance to the Prince of Peace

O Lord, you who deserve all our loyalties, we pledge allegiance this day to the Lamb of God and to the upside-down kingdom for which he stands and to the one holy nation that stands under the God who is the Servant King and the Prince of Peace, so that we may be a people who seek the liberty and justice of all without remainder. We pray this in the name of the Sovereign of all the nations of the earth. Amen.

PRAYERS FOR THE
LOVE OF NEIGHBOR

For Blessing Our Neighbor

O Lord, you who spoke your word of blessing over all of creation, may we bear your image this day by speaking a word of blessing to our neighbors, so that they might hear with their ears and feel with their hearts that you are near and not far and that you are a God of life and not of death. We pray this in the name of Jesus, the One who speaks words of life. Amen.

For Seeing the Face of Christ in Our Neighbor

O Lord, you who meet us in the face of the stranger, grant us, we pray, the heart of Veronica to see in every stranger we meet this day, whether they be hungry or thirsty, naked or sick, oppressed or in prison, the true image of Christ, worthy of service, so that we might be counted worthy of your name. We pray this in the name of Jesus, the True Icon of God. Amen.

For Kindness to a Difficult Neighbor

O Lord, you who send rain upon the righteous and the unrighteous, help me, I pray, to extend your kindness not only to my family and friends but also to my difficult neighbor, and grace me to resist the temptation to "teach them a lesson" or to "put them in their place" and instead to bless and to do good to them, so that I might be worthy to be called a child of my Father in heaven. I pray this in the name of the One who purifies all human loves. Amen.

Against Bearing False Witness

O Lord, you who come to us as the Truthful One, keep our tongues, we pray, from bearing false witness against our neighbor, guard our mouths from lies, and nourish within us a love for the truth wherever we may find it, so that we might be a people who bear your name. We pray this in the name of Jesus, the One who comes to us full of truth and grace. Amen.

For Refugees

O Lord, you who sojourned in Egypt as a refugee, may we not deprive the foreigner of justice and may we love in word and deed the stranger in our midst, we pray, so that we might become living emblems of God's neighbor love this day to the least and to the last. We pray this in the name of Jesus, the One who shows hospitality to the stranger. Amen.

For the Release of Bitterness Against One's Neighbor

O Lord, you who charge us to forgive seventy times seven, purge from me, I pray, a bitter and unforgiving spirit, help me to release all resentments to your sovereign care, and grant me the freedom to forgive my neighbor, so that I may love them as I too have been loved and forgiven. I pray this in the name of Jesus, the One who will do right by all in the end. Amen.

Against Neighbor Hate

O Lord, you who command us to bless our enemies, protect us, we pray, from turning our neighbors into enemies, worthy only of hatred and deserving of nothing but curses, and grant us instead the heart of Jesus, so that we might love our neighbor as you love them. We pray this in the name of the One who causes the sun to rise on both the evil and the good. Amen.

For Loving a Hurting Neighbor

O Lord, you who do not look away from the pain of this world, open our eyes, we pray, to see the pain of our neighbor and by God's grace to become the healing presence of the Spirit to them, so that our hearts might be kindled with your neighbor love this day. We pray this in the name of the God whose heart breaks over the troubled and helpless of this world. Amen.

For Being Generous to One's Neighbor

O Lord, you who bless the widow's mite, grant me the grace this day, I pray, to be generous-spirited in all that I say and do, and may I do so in an uncalculating manner, so that I might become tangible evidence of your economy of abundance over against a vicious economy of scarcity. I pray this in the name of Jesus, the One who multiplies the loaves and the fishes. Amen.

Against Miserliness Toward One's Neighbor

O Lord, you who rescue us from an economy of scarcity, deliver me, I pray, from a miserly heart and from the fear that you will not deal generously with me, so that I might be liberated this day to give generously to others of all that I am and have. I pray this in the joyful certainty that I have a good Father in heaven who gives generously to all his children. Amen.

For Loving Your Neighbor when You Don't Feel Like Loving Them

O Lord, you who are the True Neighbor, increase in me this day, I pray, a spirit of neighborliness and may I take joy afresh in the denial of self, so that I might bear witness to a watching world of the self-sacrificial love of Jesus. I pray this in the name of Jesus, the One who meets me in the face of my neighbor. Amen.

PRAYERS FOR
THE LOVE OF SELF

For Loving Ourself as We Have
Loved Our Neighbors

O Lord, you who command us to love our neighbors as
we love ourselves, may I not love myself any less than you
love me, I pray, so that I may honor the holy dignity of my
humanity and the beauty of the divine image that I bear
this day and always. I pray this in the name of Jesus, the
One who loves me without reserve. Amen.

For Being Patient with Oneself

O Lord, you whose love is always forbearing, forgive me, I
pray, for the ways that I have cruelly demanded of myself
things that you in your wisdom have yet to permit me to be,
and grant me the grace to be patient with myself, so that I
might experience your patient care this day. I pray this in
the name of Jesus, the Infinitely Patient One. Amen.

For Being Kind Toward Oneself

O Lord, you who are merciful and kind, forgive me, I
pray, for the ways that I have been unkind toward myself,

despising or belittling the image of God in me, and grant
me the grace to be kind to myself as you are kind to
me, so that I may experience your tender love this day. I
pray this in the name of the One who is sheer mercy and
grace. Amen.

For Not Being Proud of Oneself

O Lord, you who resist the proud but give grace to the
humble, help me, I pray, to think neither too much nor too
little of myself this day, so that I might be fully at home in
my own skin, grateful for what I am by grace, no more and
no less. I pray this in the name of the One who has made
me fearfully and wonderfully so. Amen.

For Not Dishonoring Oneself

O Lord, you who crown me with glory and honor, may
I not dishonor or deface the divine image that I bear,
whether by sins of commission or of omission against my
body and soul, I pray, so that I might glory in the beauty
and delight in the wonder of my one-of-a-kind humanity.
I pray this in the name of One who crowns me with the
brightness of Eden. Amen.

For Not Being Self-Seeking in Oneself

O Lord, you whose love is never self-seeking, help me, I
pray, not to be so full of myself that there is no room for
you to fill me up with your abundant life, so that I might

experience your more-than-enough provision for me this day. I pray this in the name of the One who generously provides for all creatures great and small. Amen.

For Not Being Easily Angered Toward Oneself

O Lord, you who are endlessly gracious, forgive me, I pray, for the ways that I have turned angry against myself, whether in violent self-castigations, unfair expectations of myself, or harmful actions toward my body, and grant me the grace instead to be compassionate with myself, so that I may abound and abide in your steadfast love this day. I pray this in the name of the Gentle One, Jesus Christ himself. Amen.

For Keeping No Record of Wrong Against Oneself

O Lord, you whose love keeps no record of wrongs, help me, I pray, neither to nurse my sins nor to replay my sins in my own mind, but rather to trust that you have removed them as far as the east is from the west, so that I might walk in the freedom of one who is wholly forgiven. I pray this in the name of the One who crowns me with love and mercy. Amen.

For Cherishing Goodness in Oneself

O Lord, you who make all things good, help me, I pray, to perceive the signs of goodness in my life and strengthen my heart to cherish these good things, so that I might not feel that only bad things mark my life or that I am only "damaged goods," but trust that your goodness will have the final word on my life. I pray this in the name of the One who calls me *very good*. Amen.

For Believing All Things

O Lord, you who remain faithful to the last, forgive me, I pray, for the ways that I have given up on myself or failed to believe that there is sufficient grace for my broken self; rescue me also from despair and indifference, so that I may bear all things, believe all things, hope all things, and endure all things, trusting that, though I may give up on myself, you will never give up on me. I pray this in the name of the One whose lovingkindness is everlasting. Amen.

PRAYERS FOR THE
LOVE OF GOD

For Learning to Pray Afresh

O Lord, you who taught the disciples to pray, teach me
afresh how to listen and not to become anxious when I
do not hear your voice; where I lack the will to pray, grant
me the grace to begin again; and where I am wordless,
let me hear the voice of your Spirit praying in me, so
that I may abide in you this day as you abide in me. I
pray this in the name of the One who stands at the right
hand of God, interceding for the saints, Jesus Christ
himself. Amen.

For Those Who Have Lost the Will to Pray

O Lord, you who have mercy upon the spent of spirit, I
confess that I have lost the will to pray, and I ask that you
would do for me what I can no longer do for myself: pray
for me. O Father, speak your word and it will be so; O
Christ, pray for me in my hour of need; O Spirit, intercede
for me with unutterable groans. I pray this so that I might
know that I have an Advocate in heaven when my heart
can no longer bear the pain of unanswered prayer. I pray

this in the name of my Sympathetic Priest whose promises
I claim this day, Jesus Christ himself. Amen.

For Those Who Struggle to Be Consistent in Prayer

O Lord, you who always welcome our weak and fickle
selves, though we remain inconstant in prayer, bless
our persistence, we pray, so that we may find you in the
struggle and meet you in the desire to desire you more. We
pray this in the name of Jesus, our Sympathetic Priest who
gladly receives all our prayers, however halfhearted or
wholehearted they may be. Amen.

For Not Wanting to Go to Church

O Lord, you who bind us together in love, how good it is
to praise your name in the congregation—except when it is
not. I confess that it is difficult to worship with your people
this day and that I often find myself frustrated and lonely
at church. Grant me the grace, I pray, to try again, so that
I might feel my kinship with your body as a joyful rather
than an onerous thing. I pray this in the name of Jesus, the
One who gladly calls us his brothers and sisters. Amen.

For the Renewal of the Church

O Spirit of God, you who unite the like and unlike, we
pray that you would reanimate our hearts with the very
resurrection life of God, attune our minds to the mind of

Christ, and bind us together in Spirited fellowship, so that we might be a sign of the Trinity to the world this day. We pray this in the name of the One who descends like fire from heaven. Amen.

For the Anxious of Heart

O Lord, you who tell us to be anxious for nothing, I confess that I am anxious for many things this day, especially for the things that I fear will hurt or disappoint me beyond anything that I could bear; speak your word of peace to my mind, I pray, of safety to my heart and of comfort to my body, so that I might know the truth, even now, that I am in the care of Another. I pray this in the name of One who daily bears my burdens. Amen.

For the Wearied and Worn Down

O Lord, you who remember that we are but dust, I confess to you my weakness of body, heart, and mind this day and I ask that you would grant me your Spirit of Life to sustain and revive me in my weakness, so that I might be renewed in this lowly and lonely place. I pray this in the name of the One who raises the dead to new life. Amen.

For Physically Separated Worship

O Spirit of God, you for whom no distance is unbridgeable, bind us together, we pray, in our worship across all our geographic divides as well as across all of our personal differences, so that we might feel keenly our kinship with one another as Christ's own body. We pray this in the name of the One who holds all things together, Jesus Christ himself. Amen.

Against Self-Deception

O Lord, you who lift my head up high, I offer up to you the whole of my life here and now: guard my heart, I pray, from self-deception, my mind from vain imaginations, my tongue from falsehood, and my soul from evil, so that I might walk in the way of integrity in all that I do and say this day. I pray this in the name of the Holy One of Israel. Amen.

For Hungering for Righteousness

O Lord, you who come to us as the Prince of Peace and the Righteous One, bless us today, we pray, with a love for peace and a hunger for righteousness in our communities, so that we might be called sons and daughters of God in the face of the discord and inequity that marks our world. We pray this in the name of the Messiah, the Son of the living God. Amen.

For Being Childlike in God's Kingdom

O Lord, you whose kingdom is upside down and not of this world, make us childlike this day, we pray, so that we might become great in your kingdom and thus brave enough to give up everything for the sake of your kingdom.

We pray this in the name of Jesus, the One who made himself nothing by taking the very nature of a servant, being made in human likeness. Amen.

For Doubting Hearts

O Lord, you who are acquainted with all my ways, search me this day, I pray, and make sense of my anxious thoughts, speak a word of hope to my doubting heart, and expose to the light any devious or self-deceptive way in my soul, so that I may walk in the way of everlasting life. I pray this in the name of the One for whom night is as bright as the day. Amen.

For the Cynics and Skeptics

O Lord, you who have mercy upon the cynics and the skeptics, open my mind, I pray, to your miraculous presence and power in the world, attune my heart to your silent stirrings within me and woo me with your tenacious love, so that I may not be overcome by my skepticism, nor be ruled by my cynicism, but with the child's father cry out, "Lord, I believe; help my unbelief!" I pray this in the name of the One who gladly gives me the gift of a childlike heart. Amen.

For Those Who Have Only a Flickering of Faith, Hope, and Love

O Lord, you who speak a mere word and things come to life, speak your creative word into my life this day, I pray, so that where there may be only a flickering of faith, hope, and love in me, your Spirit might cause these to burst into flame and call forth from me a wholehearted fervor for your name. I pray this by the power of your Creator Spirit. Amen.

Against the Temptations of the Evil One

O Lord, you who cast out demons and deliver those who have been oppressed by the devil, speak your word of disarming authority against all evil powers that would cause me to doubt your goodness in my life, I pray, so that I might be astonished afresh by your mighty deeds this day. I pray this in the name of Jesus of Nazareth. Amen.

For Those Who Are Dry in Their Souls

O Lord, you who are the ineffable sea of love and the fountain of blessing, water our hearts this day with your grace, we pray, so that we might overflow with care for our neighbors who are dry in their souls and parched in their desire for you. We pray this in the name of the One who is our Living Water, Jesus Christ himself. Amen.

For Not Giving Up on the Painful Work of Becoming Whole and Holy

O Lord, you who never give up on us, help us, we pray, not to resist or to doubt the goodness of the painful work that you are doing to make us holy and whole, so that we might yield ourselves fully to your life-giving purposes for us this day. We pray this in the name of the One who is able to accomplish abundantly far more than all we can ask or imagine. Amen.

For Those Who Feel Lost in Their Own Selves

O Lord, you who are the light of the world, be a light, I pray, to my path this day where I cannot see the way forward in my life and be a lamp in my soul where I feel lost even in my own self, so that I may sense you near at hand walking with me through the darkness. I pray this in the name of the One goes before me and who shall neither fail nor forsake me. Amen.

For Being the Light of the World

O Lord, you who are the light of the world, may the light of your countenance shine upon our face, we pray, so that we might be sons and daughters of the light, fully and freely participating in everything bright and beautiful that you have for us this day. We pray this in the name of Jesus, the One in whom there is no darkness. Amen.

For Seeing What God Sees

O Spirit of God, you who are alive and at large in the world, open my eyes this day, I pray, to perceive how you are at work around me—healing, rescuing, restoring, and reconciling—so that I might participate in the good purposes of God that you wish to perform in and through me. I pray this in the name of the One who makes dead bones rise to life. Amen.

For God's Self-Disclosure to Those Who Are in Need

O Lord, you who use not just written words and common sense but also speaking donkeys and flaming pillars to reveal yourself to your people, reveal yourself in an extraordinary way, we pray, to those who are desperate for your deliverance this day, so that they might see and believe that you are mighty to save. We pray this in the name of Jesus, our Deliverer. Amen.

For Having the Eyes and Ears of Christ

O Lord, you who heal blind eyes and deaf ears, open our eyes to see you, we pray, and open our ears to hear you, so that in seeing you we may delight to do your will and in hearing you we may trust you readily in all things that you have entrusted to us this day. We pray this in the name of the One makes us whole, Jesus Christ himself. Amen.

For Being One Hundred Percent Honest with God

O Lord, you who have searched me in order to see if there be any wicked way in me, may I stand before you, I pray, open and unafraid, fully myself and without excuses, so that I may be made holy clean and wholly alive in all that I say and do this day. I pray this in the name of the infinitely Gracious One. Amen.

Against Stingy-Heartedness

O Lord, you in whom there is more than enough, protect us, we pray, from being stingy in our words and deeds this day and grant us instead a heart of generosity, so that we might become lavish with your grace and rich in love in all that we say and do. We pray this in the name of the One who gives beyond anything that we could imagine in our wildest dreams. Amen.

For a Life of Integrity

O Lord, you who know us inside out, strengthen us, we pray, to walk with integrity before you, to do what is right by our family, to speak truth kindly to our friends and to refrain from slandering our neighbor, so that we might experience a fullness of life this day. We pray this in the name of the One who is the Forerunner of our faith, Jesus Christ himself. Amen.

For Making Forgiveness a Habit

O Lord, you who keep no record of our wrongdoings but banish them as far as the east is from the west, grant us the grace this day, we pray, to make forgiveness a habit, so that we might be freed by your forgiving love from the cancer of

resentment against our neighbor. We pray this in the name
of the One whose mercies are new every morning. Amen.

For Deliverance from All Harm

O Lord, you who are mighty to save, rescue us, we pray,
from "the world, the flesh, and the devil" this day, so that
we might be freed by your power from the snares that
would tempt us away from you and freed by your grace to
love you with all of our heart, mind, soul, and strength in
all that we do and say. We pray this through Jesus Christ
our Lord, who lives and reigns with you, in the unity of the
Holy Spirit, one God, now and forever. Amen.

For God's Judgment

O Lord, you who are a Refiner's Fire, let judgment begin
with your house this day, we pray, and let your holy fire
reveal the character of our lives, so that we may humbly
accept your scouring work in our hearts, which by grace
might lead us to true repentance and amendment of
life. We pray this in the name of the Just and Merciful
Judge. Amen.

For Being an Open Book to God

O Lord, you who put all the pieces of my life back together,
make me brave, I pray, to open up the book of my heart
to your eyes, so that you might rewrite the text of my life,
showing me the story of my truest self and freeing me to

live into my God-given calling this day. I pray this in the name of the True Storyteller, Jesus Christ himself. Amen.

For Shelter from the Storms of Life

O Lord, you who are sovereign over heaven and earth, be my refuge, I pray, and protect me from all dangers of body and soul this day, so that I might live without fear, confident that you guide my steps and will my good no matter what may come. I pray this in the name of the One who stills the storm by a single word, Jesus Christ himself. Amen.

For Vacation Bible School

O Lord, you who welcomed the little children with open arms, bless our VBS this week, we pray, as we welcome the kids into this place, that you might use us to communicate your love to each child in special and specific ways, so that each child might know that your love for them is as boundless as the sea. We pray this in the name of Jesus Christ, our Gentle Shepherd. Amen.

For the Renovation of the Heart

O Lord, you who make and mend the human heart, help me, I pray, to trust you this day with the often-painful work of renovation that you are doing in my heart, so that I might acquire the heart of Jesus and love my neighbor fully from the heart. I pray this in the name of Jesus, the One who knows and loves me wholly. Amen.

For Protection from Abandonment in the Face of the Perils of this World

O Lord, you who are the Almighty, protect us, we pray, not only from the perils of this world but also from the feelings of abandonment that would cause us to believe that we are alone in the face of such perils, so that we might find refuge under the shadow of your wings this day. We pray this in the name of Jesus, the One who never leaves or forsakes his own. Amen.

For Protection Against Our Mortal Enemy

O Lord, you who are a Mighty Warrior, help us, we pray, to remember this day that we do not fight against flesh and blood but against forces of cosmic darkness, so that we might stand firm against our mortal enemy who would steal, kill, and destroy every sign of goodness in our lives. We pray this in the name of our Strong Deliverer, Jesus Christ himself. Amen.

For Grace in the Face of Suffering

O Lord, you who learned obedience through what you suffered, may all of our suffering for your sake, we pray, become by your grace the means through which we are made wholly alive in this earthly pilgrimage, so that we might not lose heart in the hour of trial. We pray this in the name of Jesus, the One who endured the cross for joy's sake. Amen.

For Fasting

O Lord, you who fasted for forty days and forty nights, turn the hungers of my body, I pray, into a hunger for the bread that comes down from heaven and cause the thirsts of my flesh to become a thirst for the living God, so that I might know afresh that I do not live by bread alone but by every word that comes from the mouth of the Lord. I pray this in the name of Jesus, the One who sustains me in my hour of need. Amen.

For Being a Hot Mess Before God

O Lord, you whose pleasure it is always to make something out of nothing, I confess that I am a hot mess today and that I am at the end of myself; have mercy on me, I pray, and make something out of the fragmented pieces of my life, so that I might witness your life-giving power this day to mend and renew. I pray this in the name of Jesus, my Gentle Savior. Amen.

For the Love of God

O Lord, you who are the Beloved Son of your Father, may I offer my heart to you this day anew and with the psalmist say, "I love you, O Lord!" so that the love of God may fill me and form me and mark all that I do and say this day. I pray this in the name of the Spirit of God who sheds abroad the love of God in my heart. Amen.

NATURE PRAYERS

For Taking Pleasure in God's Creation

O Lord, you who are the Creator of heaven and earth, may we take pleasure in your creation this day as you take pleasure in it, we pray, and may we may live this day as a people who have been crowned with glory, so that all we do may be done in praise of you and in anticipation of that day when the whole world shall be made fully and forever alive. We pray this in the name of the One who makes heaven and earth for love's sake. Amen.

For Pets

O Lord, you who made all creatures great and small, we thank you for our pet(s) [Name]—for the joy that they bring us, the comfort that they afford us and the wonder that they show us of your creation—and we ask that you would bless them this day, that they might live a full and healthy life, and that we might care for them as you care for us, with attentive love and kindly regard. We pray this in the name of the One who makes a world teem with creatures beyond number. Amen.

For Green Spaces

O Lord, you who make us to lie down in verdant pastures, we thank you this day for the public gardens that foster community, the parks that preserve nature's beauty, and the wild places that remind us of our smallness; strengthen and inspire us, we pray, to become advocates of all such green spaces, so that all who encounter them might experience the joy of your creation. We pray this in the name of the One who makes lush meadows to grow in dry lands. Amen.

For the Feast of Saint Francis (October 4)

O Lord, you who created both leviathan and honeybee, behemoth and buzzard, cricket and dragon, maggot and mule, may we bless this day every creature that we meet along the way—whether beast of the field, bird of the air, fish of the sea, or creepy-crawly of the earth—so that we may be grateful in heart for all that you have made, both great and small. We pray this in the name of the One whose tender mercies are over all his works. Amen.

For a Bitterly Cold Morning

O Lord, you who make snow and frost, we thank you for this cold day—for the crisp air that stings the skin, the biting winds that blow from the north, and the scent of snow that lingers in the nose—and we ask that it might keep us humble in the face of your mothering nature, so that we might experience afresh the goodness of being creatures of the earth, both finite and vulnerable. We pray this in the name of the One who keeps the treasures of snow. Amen.

For a Miserably Hot Day

O Lord, you who make both cold and heat, have mercy upon us, we pray, on this miserably hot day, preserve us from irritability as we wilt and wither under the scorching heat of the sun, and help us to endure with patience the long days of summer, so that we might become attuned to the rhythms of creation and discover the grace of being slow and heavy in the heat of the day. We pray this in the name of the One who puts the sun in its place. Amen.

For Better Weather

O God, you who are the Lord of wind and wave, even as you granted Joshua, son of Nun, his request that the sun stand still and that the moon cease its turning, I ask that you would cause the weather to turn to more favorable conditions; I ask not because I am worthy but because I am desperate, so that I might rejoice rather than be miserable this day. In pray this in the name of the One who will do right by the whole earth. Amen.

For the Winter Solstice

O Lord, you for whom the night is bright as the day, we thank you for the gift of this long night—for the deep quiet of the earth, the long sleep of creatures beneath the earth, and the stars that shine brightly above the earth—and we ask that you would keep us in your care as we watch for the rising of the sun over the horizon of the earth, so that we might be a people who wait in hope. We pray this in the name of Jesus, our Bright Morning Star. Amen.

For the Summer Solstice

O Lord, you who are the light of the world, we thank you for this long day—for its expansive light, its radiant warmth, its generative vigor, and the fierce power of the sun—and we ask that your light might shine upon us and bless us this day, so that we might be a people who bring out the God-colors in the world. We pray this in the name of Jesus, the Light of Light. Amen.

Against Raging Hurricane Storms

O Lord, you who stand sovereign over wind and wave, be with us this day, we pray, in the face of storms that savage the land and winds that swallow up home and hope; do not be deaf to our cries but be the God of life from death, we pray, near to the brokenhearted and empty-handed, so that we may experience you this day as the God who brings order out of chaos. We pray this in the name of the One who is our Shelter and Shield. Amen.

Against Raging Forest Fires

O Lord, you who govern all forces of nature, have mercy, we pray, upon the lands that have been ravaged by fire;

quench the fires that consume the forests, douse the flame that sets the mountains ablaze, shield the weak and take pity upon all creatures, great and small, so that the land might rest from its turmoil and we might praise your mighty name. We pray this in the name of the One who safely carries his people through fire and water. Amen.

Against Raging Earthquakes

O Lord, you who are an ever-present help in the time of trouble, have mercy, we pray, upon the people who have suffered an earthquake this day; silence the spasms of the earth and still the tremors beneath the earth, so that they might be rescued in the day of their disaster and be comforted by your Spirit in the losses of life and home. We pray this in the name of the One who is the Repairer of Broken Walls and the Restorer of Streets with Dwellings. Amen.

For the Care of Creation

O Lord, you who made us to till and to keep the earth, grace us, we pray, to preserve its beauty and to protect it against harm as well as to delight in all of its variety and to steward all of its riches, so that we might care for it as you care for it, in wisdom and in love. We pray this for your sake and our neighbor's as well, both near and far. We pray this in the name of the One who sustains all of creation, Jesus Christ himself. Amen.

CHILDREN'S PRAYERS

For God's Shepherding Care

O God, my Shepherd,
My Guide and my Guard,
Be with me this day,
And hear me, I pray.

When I'm low: lift me up.
When I'm dry: fill my cup.
When I'm weak: make me strong.
This, I pray, all day long.

Here and there,
In your certain care,
My strength, my shield,
My hope and my prayer.

O God, my Shepherd,
My Guide and my Guard,
Bless me, this day,
And hear me, I pray.

For Waking Up on the Wrong Side of the Bed

New mercies each morning is what you sure said,
But I woke up today on the wrong side of bed.
I'm grumpy and grouchy and tired and mad;
An "attitude" (they call it)—and it's really bad.

Please help me to change and help it to stick,
A heart that is soft and gentle and quick;
To say "thank you" and "please" and "let's try again,"
So today by your grace might come to a good end.

For Bedtime

Sweet Jesus, Sweet Lord,
Be near me this night.
Be with me,
Here for me,
Secure in your might.

Your angels to guard,
Your power to ward,
My fears keep at bay,
For this do I pray.

Sweet Jesus, Sweet Lord,
In mind and in heart,
Surround me,

Support me,
Your peace do impart.

You call me "beloved,"
And sweet blessed friend.
In peace do I sleep,
A sweet gift, amen.

For Anxious Children at Bedtime

My Good Shepherd, shepherd me
Hear my prayer and my plea
May I sleep in peace tonight
In your warm and shielding light

Help me not to feel alone
Be my refuge and my home
Please protect my heart from fear
And to trust that you are near

Guard me from all things that harm
And enfold me in your arms
Thank you, Lord, for your sweet care
And for hearing this my prayer

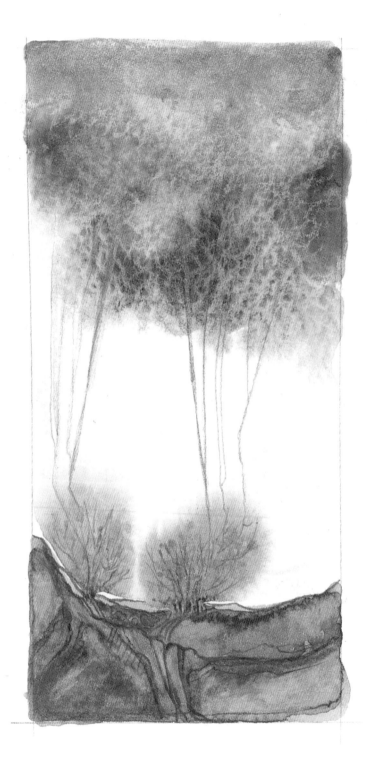

CELTIC PRAYERS

For a Blessing of the Day

Holy God, Holy Trinity,
Bless me this day, I pray:

Bless my thinking, bless my feeling;
Bless my speaking, bless my hearing;
Bless my knowing, bless my doing;
Bless my going, bless my coming;
Bless my working, bless my resting.

Bless me, O Father, and all who are dear to me.
Bless me, O Spirit, in all that I hear and see.
Bless me, O Christ, and all who are near to me.

Bless me, O God, the Godhead Three,
Your blessing, O God, upon me be.

For the Morning

O Lord, my body and soul
To you I commend this day:

I rise from my bed this day
by your grace;
I face the tasks of this day
by your grace;
I embrace the turns of this day
by your grace;
I receive the gifts of this day
by your grace;
I hold lightly the end of this day
by your grace.

In the name of the One
Who comes to me, I pray,
The God beyond measure,
Full of grace beyond grace,
I commend soul and body
To his grace this whole day.

For Commending Ourselves Wholly to Christ

This moment, however fleeting, be yours, O Christ.
This hour, however brief, be yours, O Christ.
This day, however fickle, be yours, O Christ.
My life, however long, be yours, O Christ.
May I be your own and you ever be mine,
This day and forever, I pray, O Christ.

For Being the Limbs of Christ

Incarnate God, Word made Flesh:
Use my hands, I pray,
To bring a healing touch to those
whose bodies are in pain this day;

Incarnate God, Word made Flesh:
Use my feet, I pray,
To bring a word of peace to those
who are at war with themselves this day;

Incarnate God, Word made Flesh:
Use my mouth, I pray,
To speak a word of hope to those
who despair this day;

Incarnate God, Word made Flesh:
Use my ears, I pray,
To be hearing ears to those
who need to come clean this day.

Incarnate God, Word made Flesh:
Be pleased to be
My hands and my feet
My eyes and my ears
My mouth and my tongue
To be a messenger of your own Body this day.

For Marriages

Guard, O Father, my marriage this day,
Guard it, I pray.
Nourish, O Christ, my marriage this day,
Nourish it, I pray.
Gladden, O Spirit, my marriage this day,
Gladden it, I pray.
That I may bless her/him
And he/she bless me,
And we bless all we meet this day.
This day and forever more, we pray.

For Commending Our Night to Christ

Into your care, O Christ, I pray,
I commend all that occurred this day:

My leaving,
My returning,
My giving,
My receiving,
My speaking,
My hearing,
My doing,
My ceasing,
My rising,
My resting.

Bless me this night, O Christ,
That I may sleep in peace
And from my labors cease,
To arise in grace
And a new day face,
In your warm embrace,
O Christ, O God of grace.

To the Holy Trinity

Holy God, Living God:
Fill me with your life this day.
Holy God, Saving God:
Keep me from all harm this day.
Holy God, Healing God:
Make me whole anew this day.
Holy God, Serving God:
Strengthen hand and feet this day.
Holy God, Triune God:
Bring me to good end this day.

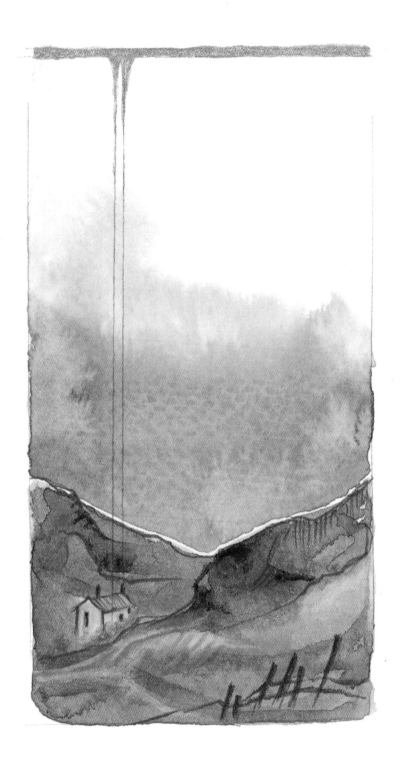

A PRAYER FOR THE NOBODIES OF THE WORLD

O Lord, you who delight to announce the birth of Jesus,
not to professional heralds of the empire,
capable of spreading the news
to the largest number of people
—people of influence and sophistication
who know how to get things done,
to produce maximally effective results,
generating thereby the greatest amount of good
for the greatest number of people—
but rather to a trivial number of shepherds,
the nobodies of the world,
rude, rough, and easily forgettable,
to whom an excessive number of angels
sing an exquisitely composed anthem
in the lower atmosphere
(a Fanfare for the Common Man, they called it),
who spread the news throughout the
all-too-little town of Bethlehem,
not to one of those "Cities of the Future,"
stirring the hearts of a few souls,
impressing a handful of night creatures,

then returning to their day jobs, near dawn,
back to the grind of their small and simple lives.
May we, like you, delight to give extravagantly
of ourselves and of our goods
to the least and to the last,
to the lowest and to the lost,
even to those who may not appreciate our gift
but who nonetheless deserve the best and the finest,
so that we might acquire a heart of generosity
that knows no bounds,
which gives without expectation of return,
which gives in joy because we know to whom belong:
to a generous Father in heaven
who owns the cattle on a thousand hills,
whose Son generates an excess of wine
and a surfeit of bread,
exceeding all requirements of necessity,
and whose Spirit floods our hearts
with the abundant love of God,
with a love that loves us to the end,
so that we might become emissaries
of God's gracious bounty
in a world that dares us to believe otherwise.
We pray this in the name of the One
who makes us rich by becoming poor for our sake.
We pray this in the name of the Father, the Son, and the
Holy Spirit.
Amen.

ACKNOWLEDGMENTS

Our sincerest thanks to Ethan McCarthy for believing in this project and for supporting it to its completion. And to the team at InterVarsity Press more generally, our deepest gratitude not just for partnering with us on this book but also for producing such a beautiful object—and for believing that Phaedra's full-color paintings were worth the investment. We wish also to express our thanks to Shannon Coelho and Sarah Smith for their generous and perspicacious feedback on the manuscript. And to the parents and children at Church of the Cross who provided feedback on the prayers for kids: thank you a million. It is also the case that without Pete Peterson's willingness to produce our illustrated prayer cards through the Rabbit Room Press back in the spring of 2020, and two other subsequent sets, I don't think we would have believed that this book was possible or desirable, so to him and to the Rabbit Room community more broadly go our wholehearted gratitude. We do not take for granted our friendship with you. Neither do we take for granted the dear saints at Hope Chapel in Austin, Texas, who prayed for us in the hours of our need, who taught us how to pray and to love the life of prayer, and who modeled for us the gift and grace of a praying community all those years ago. Finally, we could not have arrived at this place apart from the continual encouragement, lively engagement, and recurring requests for prayers from friends and strangers over social media. Our heartfelt thanks to each and every one of you—and to fellow pilgrims like you. May this book of prayers bless you from head to toe and inside out.

Appendix

HOW TO WRITE YOUR OWN COLLECTS

One of the assignments that I have given to my students at Fuller Theological Seminary over the years is to write a weekly collect. I suggest that if they wish to understand the basic grammar of Christian prayer, they need to immerse themselves in praying the Lord's Prayer (the New Testament prayer), the Psalms (the Old Testament prayer), and collects (the prayer of church history).

A collect is most fundamentally a commemorative prayer. It intends to bring to mind what God has done in the past and invites us to remember who God will continue to be in the present in the prayers that we pray; hence the "you who" pattern of this particular form of prayer.

Doing this well requires that we immerse ourselves in the stories and details of the Bible. By invoking the name of God in light of a particular activity of God that we witness in Scripture, we protect ourselves from abstract or idiosyncratic ideas of divine justice, for example, or divine love, and instead root such ideas in the concrete expression of how the Holy Trinity does justice and love, and so on.

The basic structure of the collect is relatively straightforward, but it also involves a very specific logic:

- Begin by naming God.
- Remember God's activities or attributes.
- State your request of God.
- State your desired hope for such a request.
- End by naming God again.

One of the best parts of the collect, as I often tell my students, is that while prescriptive in form, it lends itself easily to extemporaneous expression. There is no circumstance in life where this prayer cannot become immediately useful. So I give my students a range of themes and topics in order to practice writing their own collects.

Anybody can write a collect, really: individuals, small groups, church staff, community leaders, teachers, coaches, therapists, spiritual directors, even children. All that's needed is to learn the form, to become familiar with the landscape and language of Holy Scripture, and to imagine circumstances or needs that are relevant to your life.

May God bless you, then, as you try writing your own collects, and may God bless those who receive your prayers.

The nautilus is one of the sea's oldest creatures. Beginning with a tight center, its remarkable growth pattern can be seen in the ever-enlarging chambers that spiral outward. The nautilus in the IVP Formatio logo symbolizes deep inward work of spiritual formation that begins rooted in our souls and then opens to the world as we experience spiritual transformation. The shell takes on a stunning pearlized appearance as it ages and forms in much the same way as the souls of those who devote themselves to spiritual practice. Formatio books draw on the ancient wisdom of the saints and the early church as well as the rich resources of Scripture, applying tradition to the needs of contemporary life and practice.

Within each of us is a longing to be in God's presence. Formatio books call us into our deepest desires and help us to become our true selves in the light of God's grace.

VISIT

ivpress.com/formatio

to see all of the books in the line and to sign up for the IVP Formatio newsletter.

Like this book?

Scan the code to discover more content like this!

Get on IVP's email list to receive special offers, exclusive book news, and thoughtful content from your favorite authors on topics you care about.

 InterVarsity Press